C-4990 CAREER EXAMINATION SERIES

This is your
PASSBOOK® for...

Postal Virtual Entry Assessment Tests (USPS)

Test Preparation Study Guide
Questions & Answers

NATIONAL LEARNING CORPORATION®

COPYRIGHT NOTICE

This book is SOLELY intended for, is sold ONLY to, and its use is RESTRICTED to individual, bona fide applicants or candidates who qualify by virtue of having seriously filed applications for appropriate license, certificate, professional and/or promotional advancement, higher school matriculation, scholarship, or other legitimate requirements of education and/or governmental authorities.

This book is NOT intended for use, class instruction, tutoring, training, duplication, copying, reprinting, excerption, or adaptation, etc., by:

1) Other publishers
2) Proprietors and/or Instructors of "Coaching" and/or Preparatory Courses
3) Personnel and/or Training Divisions of commercial, industrial, and governmental organizations
4) Schools, colleges, or universities and/or their departments and staffs, including teachers and other personnel
5) Testing Agencies or Bureaus
6) Study groups which seek by the purchase of a single volume to copy and/or duplicate and/or adapt this material for use by the group as a whole without having purchased individual volumes for each of the members of the group
7) Et al.

Such persons would be in violation of appropriate Federal and State statutes.

PROVISION OF LICENSING AGREEMENTS – Recognized educational, commercial, industrial, and governmental institutions and organizations, and others legitimately engaged in educational pursuits, including training, testing, and measurement activities, may address request for a licensing agreement to the copyright owners, who will determine whether, and under what conditions, including fees and charges, the materials in this book may be used them. In other words, a licensing facility exists for the legitimate use of the material in this book on other than an individual basis. However, it is asseverated and affirmed here that the material in this book CANNOT be used without the receipt of the express permission of such a licensing agreement from the Publishers. Inquiries re licensing should be addressed to the company, attention rights and permissions department.

All rights reserved, including the right of reproduction in whole or in part, in any form or by any means, electronic or mechanical, including photocopying, recording, or by any information storage and retrieval system, without permission in writing from the Publisher.

Copyright © 2024 by
National Learning Corporation

212 Michael Drive, Syosset, NY 11791
(516) 921-8888 • www.passbooks.com
E-mail: info@passbooks.com

PUBLISHED IN THE UNITED STATES OF AMERICA

PASSBOOK® SERIES

THE *PASSBOOK® SERIES* has been created to prepare applicants and candidates for the ultimate academic battlefield – the examination room.

At some time in our lives, each and every one of us may be required to take an examination – for validation, matriculation, admission, qualification, registration, certification, or licensure.

Based on the assumption that every applicant or candidate has met the basic formal educational standards, has taken the required number of courses, and read the necessary texts, the *PASSBOOK® SERIES* furnishes the one special preparation which may assure passing with confidence, instead of failing with insecurity. Examination questions – together with answers – are furnished as the basic vehicle for study so that the mysteries of the examination and its compounding difficulties may be eliminated or diminished by a sure method.

This book is meant to help you pass your examination provided that you qualify and are serious in your objective.

The entire field is reviewed through the huge store of content information which is succinctly presented through a provocative and challenging approach – the question-and-answer method.

A climate of success is established by furnishing the correct answers at the end of each test.

You soon learn to recognize types of questions, forms of questions, and patterns of questioning. You may even begin to anticipate expected outcomes.

You perceive that many questions are repeated or adapted so that you can gain acute insights, which may enable you to score many sure points.

You learn how to confront new questions, or types of questions, and to attack them confidently and work out the correct answers.

You note objectives and emphases, and recognize pitfalls and dangers, so that you may make positive educational adjustments.

Moreover, you are kept fully informed in relation to new concepts, methods, practices, and directions in the field.

You discover that you are actually taking the examination all the time: you are preparing for the examination by "taking" an examination, not by reading extraneous and/or supererogatory textbooks.

In short, this PASSBOOK®, used directedly, should be an important factor in helping you to pass your test.

VIRTUAL ENTRY ASSESSMENT TESTS
UNITED STATES POSTAL SERVICE

The Virtual Entry Assessment Tests are online assessments used by the United States Postal Service (USPS) to screen candidates for various positions. In April 2019, the USPS replaced Postal Exam 473 with four new exams:

- **Virtual Entry Assessment MC (474) - for Mail Carrier jobs**
- **Virtual Entry Assessment MH (475) - for Mail Handler jobs**
- **Virtual Entry Assessment MP (476) - for Mail Processing jobs**
- **Virtual Entry Assessment CS (477) - for Customer Service Clerk jobs**

The passing score for any of the four VEA tests is 70. Candidates who fail to reach the minimum score of 70 can retake the exam after one year. It is important to score as highly as possible (maximum score is 100) because candidates who achieve a passing score of 70 but do not get hired are ineligible to retake the exam for two years.

Virtual Entry Assessment Tests are self-administered and must be completed within three days of applying for a USPS job. Test results for each of the four assessments are used to fill a variety of Postal Service positions. For instance, scores on the Mail Carrier 474 exam will screen candidates for different levels of City Carrier and Rural Carrier jobs.

Virtual Entry Assessment MC (474)

Virtual Entry Assessment MC (474) is used for evaluating candidates applying for both City and Rural Carrier positions. The 474 exam is structured as follows:

Section Name	Number of Questions	Time Limit (approx.)
Work Scenarios (Situational Judgment)	9	7 minutes
Tell Us Your Story (Biodata Questionnaire)	20	2 minutes
Describe Your Approach (Personality Test)	56	6 minutes

SAMPLE QUESTION

Work Scenarios (Situational Judgment)
You are carrying mail outside an apartment building when a resident asks for the address of a nearby restaurant. He is not sure how to locate this information but inquired with the assumption you are familiar with the neighborhood.

Select the course of action you would most likely take in the work scenario described above.

  A. Tell him he can find that information on a simple internet search
  B. Explain where he may find this information and follow up to see if he found it
  C. Offer to help him search for the address on the USPS website
  D. Tell him where he can find this information and ask if you can help in any other way

Virtual Entry Assessment MH (475)

Virtual Entry Assessment MH 475 is an exam for candidates looking to become a USPS Mail Handler or Mail Handler Assistant. The 475 exam is structured as follows:

Section Name	Number of Questions	Time Limit (approx.)
Work Scenarios (Situational Judgment)	9	11 minutes
Check for Errors	12	2 minutes
Tell Us Your Story (Biodata Questionnaire)	22	3 minutes
Describe Your Approach	79	8 minutes

SAMPLE QUESTION

Check For Errors
Choose the option (A, B, C, or D) with the identification number and name that EXACTLY matches the number and name provided.

981121 Phillip M. Maas

  A. 981121 Phillip M. Mass
  B. 981211 Phillip M. Maas
  C. 981121 Phillip M. Maas
  D. 981121 Phillip N. Maas

Virtual Entry Assessment MP (476)

Virtual Entry Assessment MP 476 is used in the screening process for many roles related to Mail Processing, such as Clerks and Conversion Operators. The 476 exam is structured as follows:

Section Name	Number of Questions	Time Limit (approx.)
Work Scenarios (Situational Judgment)	9	11 minutes
Check for Errors	12	2 minutes
Tell Us Your Story (Biodata Questionnaire)	22	3 minutes
Describe Your Approach	79	8 minutes

SAMPLE QUESTION

Tell Us Your Story (Biodata Questionnaire)
After completing an important project ahead of schedule, which of the following gives you the GREATEST satisfaction?

   A. Being told you have done a good job.
   B. Providing a solution that helps others.
   C. Innovating a new way to carry out or manage a project.
   D. Having free time to devote to personal interests.

Virtual Entry Assessment CS (477)

Virtual Entry Assessment CS 477 is used to screen candidates for retail customer service jobs at the Post Office. The 477 exam is structured as follows:

Section Name	Number of Questions	Time Limit (approx.)
Work Scenarios (Situational Judgment)	10	8 minutes
Work Your Register	3	2 minutes
Tell Us Your Story (Biodata Questionnaire)	21	2 minutes
Describe Your Approach	56	6 minutes

SAMPLE QUESTION

Work Your Register
A customer hands you a $5 bill to pay for postage totaling $1.30. What is the CORRECT change listed below that you should give to the customer?

   D. No change should be given

HOW TO TAKE A TEST

I. YOU MUST PASS AN EXAMINATION

A. *WHAT EVERY CANDIDATE SHOULD KNOW*

Examination applicants often ask us for help in preparing for the written test. What can I study in advance? What kinds of questions will be asked? How will the test be given? How will the papers be graded?

As an applicant for a civil service examination, you may be wondering about some of these things. Our purpose here is to suggest effective methods of advance study and to describe civil service examinations.

Your chances for success on this examination can be increased if you know how to prepare. Those "pre-examination jitters" can be reduced if you know what to expect. You can even experience an adventure in good citizenship if you know why civil service exams are given.

B. *WHY ARE CIVIL SERVICE EXAMINATIONS GIVEN?*

Civil service examinations are important to you in two ways. As a citizen, you want public jobs filled by employees who know how to do their work. As a job seeker, you want a fair chance to compete for that job on an equal footing with other candidates. The best-known means of accomplishing this two-fold goal is the competitive examination.

Exams are widely publicized throughout the nation. They may be administered for jobs in federal, state, city, municipal, town or village governments or agencies.

Any citizen may apply, with some limitations, such as the age or residence of applicants. Your experience and education may be reviewed to see whether you meet the requirements for the particular examination. When these requirements exist, they are reasonable and applied consistently to all applicants. Thus, a competitive examination may cause you some uneasiness now, but it is your privilege and safeguard.

C. *HOW ARE CIVIL SERVICE EXAMS DEVELOPED?*

Examinations are carefully written by trained technicians who are specialists in the field known as "psychological measurement," in consultation with recognized authorities in the field of work that the test will cover. These experts recommend the subject matter areas or skills to be tested; only those knowledges or skills important to your success on the job are included. The most reliable books and source materials available are used as references. Together, the experts and technicians judge the difficulty level of the questions.

Test technicians know how to phrase questions so that the problem is clearly stated. Their ethics do not permit "trick" or "catch" questions. Questions may have been tried out on sample groups, or subjected to statistical analysis, to determine their usefulness.

Written tests are often used in combination with performance tests, ratings of training and experience, and oral interviews. All of these measures combine to form the best-known means of finding the right person for the right job.

II. HOW TO PASS THE WRITTEN TEST

A. NATURE OF THE EXAMINATION

To prepare intelligently for civil service examinations, you should know how they differ from school examinations you have taken. In school you were assigned certain definite pages to read or subjects to cover. The examination questions were quite detailed and usually emphasized memory. Civil service exams, on the other hand, try to discover your present ability to perform the duties of a position, plus your potentiality to learn these duties. In other words, a civil service exam attempts to predict how successful you will be. Questions cover such a broad area that they cannot be as minute and detailed as school exam questions.

In the public service similar kinds of work, or positions, are grouped together in one "class." This process is known as *position-classification*. All the positions in a class are paid according to the salary range for that class. One class title covers all of these positions, and they are all tested by the same examination.

B. FOUR BASIC STEPS

1) Study the announcement

How, then, can you know what subjects to study? Our best answer is: "Learn as much as possible about the class of positions for which you've applied." The exam will test the knowledge, skills and abilities needed to do the work.

Your most valuable source of information about the position you want is the official exam announcement. This announcement lists the training and experience qualifications. Check these standards and apply only if you come reasonably close to meeting them.

The brief description of the position in the examination announcement offers some clues to the subjects which will be tested. Think about the job itself. Review the duties in your mind. Can you perform them, or are there some in which you are rusty? Fill in the blank spots in your preparation.

Many jurisdictions preview the written test in the exam announcement by including a section called "Knowledge and Abilities Required," "Scope of the Examination," or some similar heading. Here you will find out specifically what fields will be tested.

2) Review your own background

Once you learn in general what the position is all about, and what you need to know to do the work, ask yourself which subjects you already know fairly well and which need improvement. You may wonder whether to concentrate on improving your strong areas or on building some background in your fields of weakness. When the announcement has specified "some knowledge" or "considerable knowledge," or has used adjectives like "beginning principles of..." or "advanced ... methods," you can get a clue as to the number and difficulty of questions to be asked in any given field. More questions, and hence broader coverage, would be included for those subjects which are more important in the work. Now weigh your strengths and weaknesses against the job requirements and prepare accordingly.

3) Determine the level of the position

Another way to tell how intensively you should prepare is to understand the level of the job for which you are applying. Is it the entering level? In other words, is this the position in which beginners in a field of work are hired? Or is it an intermediate or advanced level? Sometimes this is indicated by such words as "Junior" or "Senior" in the class title. Other jurisdictions use Roman numerals to designate the level – Clerk I, Clerk II, for example. The word "Supervisor" sometimes appears in the title. If the level is not indicated by the title, check the description of duties. Will you be working under very close supervision, or will you have responsibility for independent decisions in this work?

4) Choose appropriate study materials

Now that you know the subjects to be examined and the relative amount of each subject to be covered, you can choose suitable study materials. For beginning level jobs, or even advanced ones, if you have a pronounced weakness in some aspect of your training, read a modern, standard textbook in that field. Be sure it is up to date and has general coverage. Such books are normally available at your library, and the librarian will be glad to help you locate one. For entry-level positions, questions of appropriate difficulty are chosen -- neither highly advanced questions, nor those too simple. Such questions require careful thought but not advanced training.

If the position for which you are applying is technical or advanced, you will read more advanced, specialized material. If you are already familiar with the basic principles of your field, elementary textbooks would waste your time. Concentrate on advanced textbooks and technical periodicals. Think through the concepts and review difficult problems in your field.

These are all general sources. You can get more ideas on your own initiative, following these leads. For example, training manuals and publications of the government agency which employs workers in your field can be useful, particularly for technical and professional positions. A letter or visit to the government department involved may result in more specific study suggestions, and certainly will provide you with a more definite idea of the exact nature of the position you are seeking.

III. KINDS OF TESTS

Tests are used for purposes other than measuring knowledge and ability to perform specified duties. For some positions, it is equally important to test ability to make adjustments to new situations or to profit from training. In others, basic mental abilities not dependent on information are essential. Questions which test these things may not appear as pertinent to the duties of the position as those which test for knowledge and information. Yet they are often highly important parts of a fair examination. For very general questions, it is almost impossible to help you direct your study efforts. What we can do is to point out some of the more common of these general abilities needed in public service positions and describe some typical questions.

1) General information

Broad, general information has been found useful for predicting job success in some kinds of work. This is tested in a variety of ways, from vocabulary lists to questions about current events. Basic background in some field of work, such as sociology or economics, may be sampled in a group of questions. Often these are principles which have become familiar to most persons through exposure rather than through formal training. It is difficult to advise you how to study for these questions; being alert to the world around you is our best suggestion.

2) Verbal ability

An example of an ability needed in many positions is verbal or language ability. Verbal ability is, in brief, the ability to use and understand words. Vocabulary and grammar tests are typical measures of this ability. Reading comprehension or paragraph interpretation questions are common in many kinds of civil service tests. You are given a paragraph of written material and asked to find its central meaning.

3) Numerical ability

Number skills can be tested by the familiar arithmetic problem, by checking paired lists of numbers to see which are alike and which are different, or by interpreting charts and graphs. In the latter test, a graph may be printed in the test booklet which you are asked to use as the basis for answering questions.

4) Observation

A popular test for law-enforcement positions is the observation test. A picture is shown to you for several minutes, then taken away. Questions about the picture test your ability to observe both details and larger elements.

5) Following directions

In many positions in the public service, the employee must be able to carry out written instructions dependably and accurately. You may be given a chart with several columns, each column listing a variety of information. The questions require you to carry out directions involving the information given in the chart.

6) Skills and aptitudes

Performance tests effectively measure some manual skills and aptitudes. When the skill is one in which you are trained, such as typing or shorthand, you can practice. These tests are often very much like those given in business school or high school courses. For many of the other skills and aptitudes, however, no short-time preparation can be made. Skills and abilities natural to you or that you have developed throughout your lifetime are being tested.

Many of the general questions just described provide all the data needed to answer the questions and ask you to use your reasoning ability to find the answers. Your best preparation for these tests, as well as for tests of facts and ideas, is to be at your physical and mental best. You, no doubt, have your own methods of getting into an exam-taking mood and keeping "in shape." The next section lists some ideas on this subject.

IV. KINDS OF QUESTIONS

Only rarely is the "essay" question, which you answer in narrative form, used in civil service tests. Civil service tests are usually of the short-answer type. Full instructions for answering these questions will be given to you at the examination. But in case this is your first experience with short-answer questions and separate answer sheets, here is what you need to know:

1) Multiple-choice Questions

Most popular of the short-answer questions is the "multiple choice" or "best answer" question. It can be used, for example, to test for factual knowledge, ability to solve problems or judgment in meeting situations found at work.

A multiple-choice question is normally one of three types—
- It can begin with an incomplete statement followed by several possible endings. You are to find the one ending which *best* completes the statement, although some of the others may not be entirely wrong.
- It can also be a complete statement in the form of a question which is answered by choosing one of the statements listed.

- It can be in the form of a problem – again you select the best answer.

Here is an example of a multiple-choice question with a discussion which should give you some clues as to the method for choosing the right answer:

When an employee has a complaint about his assignment, the action which will *best* help him overcome his difficulty is to
- A. discuss his difficulty with his coworkers
- B. take the problem to the head of the organization
- C. take the problem to the person who gave him the assignment
- D. say nothing to anyone about his complaint

In answering this question, you should study each of the choices to find which is best. Consider choice "A" – Certainly an employee may discuss his complaint with fellow employees, but no change or improvement can result, and the complaint remains unresolved. Choice "B" is a poor choice since the head of the organization probably does not know what assignment you have been given, and taking your problem to him is known as "going over the head" of the supervisor. The supervisor, or person who made the assignment, is the person who can clarify it or correct any injustice. Choice "C" is, therefore, correct. To say nothing, as in choice "D," is unwise. Supervisors have and interest in knowing the problems employees are facing, and the employee is seeking a solution to his problem.

2) True/False Questions

The "true/false" or "right/wrong" form of question is sometimes used. Here a complete statement is given. Your job is to decide whether the statement is right or wrong.

SAMPLE: A roaming cell-phone call to a nearby city costs less than a non-roaming call to a distant city.

This statement is wrong, or false, since roaming calls are more expensive.

This is not a complete list of all possible question forms, although most of the others are variations of these common types. You will always get complete directions for answering questions. Be sure you understand *how* to mark your answers – ask questions until you do.

V. RECORDING YOUR ANSWERS

Computer terminals are used more and more today for many different kinds of exams.
For an examination with very few applicants, you may be told to record your answers in the test booklet itself. Separate answer sheets are much more common. If this separate answer sheet is to be scored by machine – and this is often the case – it is highly important that you mark your answers correctly in order to get credit.
An electronic scoring machine is often used in civil service offices because of the speed with which papers can be scored. Machine-scored answer sheets must be marked with a pencil, which will be given to you. This pencil has a high graphite content which responds to the electronic scoring machine. As a matter of fact, stray dots may register as answers, so do not let your pencil rest on the answer sheet while you are pondering the correct answer. Also, if your pencil lead breaks or is otherwise defective, ask for another.

Since the answer sheet will be dropped in a slot in the scoring machine, be careful not to bend the corners or get the paper crumpled.

The answer sheet normally has five vertical columns of numbers, with 30 numbers to a column. These numbers correspond to the question numbers in your test booklet. After each number, going across the page are four or five pairs of dotted lines. These short dotted lines have small letters or numbers above them. The first two pairs may also have a "T" or "F" above the letters. This indicates that the first two pairs only are to be used if the questions are of the true-false type. If the questions are multiple choice, disregard the "T" and "F" and pay attention only to the small letters or numbers.

Answer your questions in the manner of the sample that follows:

   32. The largest city in the United States is
       A. Washington, D.C.
       B. New York City
       C. Chicago
       D. Detroit
       E. San Francisco

1) Choose the answer you think is best. (New York City is the largest, so "B" is correct.)
2) Find the row of dotted lines numbered the same as the question you are answering. (Find row number 32)
3) Find the pair of dotted lines corresponding to the answer. (Find the pair of lines under the mark "B.")
4) Make a solid black mark between the dotted lines.

VI. BEFORE THE TEST

Common sense will help you find procedures to follow to get ready for an examination. Too many of us, however, overlook these sensible measures. Indeed, nervousness and fatigue have been found to be the most serious reasons why applicants fail to do their best on civil service tests. Here is a list of reminders:

- Begin your preparation early – Don't wait until the last minute to go scurrying around for books and materials or to find out what the position is all about.
- Prepare continuously – An hour a night for a week is better than an all-night cram session. This has been definitely established. What is more, a night a week for a month will return better dividends than crowding your study into a shorter period of time.
- Locate the place of the exam – You have been sent a notice telling you when and where to report for the examination. If the location is in a different town or otherwise unfamiliar to you, it would be well to inquire the best route and learn something about the building.
- Relax the night before the test – Allow your mind to rest. Do not study at all that night. Plan some mild recreation or diversion; then go to bed early and get a good night's sleep.
- Get up early enough to make a leisurely trip to the place for the test – This way unforeseen events, traffic snarls, unfamiliar buildings, etc. will not upset you.
- Dress comfortably – A written test is not a fashion show. You will be known by number and not by name, so wear something comfortable.

- Leave excess paraphernalia at home – Shopping bags and odd bundles will get in your way. You need bring only the items mentioned in the official notice you received; usually everything you need is provided. Do not bring reference books to the exam. They will only confuse those last minutes and be taken away from you when in the test room.
- Arrive somewhat ahead of time – If because of transportation schedules you must get there very early, bring a newspaper or magazine to take your mind off yourself while waiting.
- Locate the examination room – When you have found the proper room, you will be directed to the seat or part of the room where you will sit. Sometimes you are given a sheet of instructions to read while you are waiting. Do not fill out any forms until you are told to do so; just read them and be prepared.
- Relax and prepare to listen to the instructions
- If you have any physical problem that may keep you from doing your best, be sure to tell the test administrator. If you are sick or in poor health, you really cannot do your best on the exam. You can come back and take the test some other time.

VII. AT THE TEST

The day of the test is here and you have the test booklet in your hand. The temptation to get going is very strong. Caution! There is more to success than knowing the right answers. You must know how to identify your papers and understand variations in the type of short-answer question used in this particular examination. Follow these suggestions for maximum results from your efforts:

1) Cooperate with the monitor

The test administrator has a duty to create a situation in which you can be as much at ease as possible. He will give instructions, tell you when to begin, check to see that you are marking your answer sheet correctly, and so on. He is not there to guard you, although he will see that your competitors do not take unfair advantage. He wants to help you do your best.

2) Listen to all instructions

Don't jump the gun! Wait until you understand all directions. In most civil service tests you get more time than you need to answer the questions. So don't be in a hurry. Read each word of instructions until you clearly understand the meaning. Study the examples, listen to all announcements and follow directions. Ask questions if you do not understand what to do.

3) Identify your papers

Civil service exams are usually identified by number only. You will be assigned a number; you must not put your name on your test papers. Be sure to copy your number correctly. Since more than one exam may be given, copy your exact examination title.

4) Plan your time

Unless you are told that a test is a "speed" or "rate of work" test, speed itself is usually not important. Time enough to answer all the questions will be provided, but this does not mean that you have all day. An overall time limit has been set. Divide the total time (in minutes) by the number of questions to determine the approximate time you have for each question.

5) Do not linger over difficult questions

If you come across a difficult question, mark it with a paper clip (useful to have along) and come back to it when you have been through the booklet. One caution if you do this – be sure to skip a number on your answer sheet as well. Check often to be sure that you have not lost your place and that you are marking in the row numbered the same as the question you are answering.

6) Read the questions

Be sure you know what the question asks! Many capable people are unsuccessful because they failed to *read* the questions correctly.

7) Answer all questions

Unless you have been instructed that a penalty will be deducted for incorrect answers, it is better to guess than to omit a question.

8) Speed tests

It is often better NOT to guess on speed tests. It has been found that on timed tests people are tempted to spend the last few seconds before time is called in marking answers at random – without even reading them – in the hope of picking up a few extra points. To discourage this practice, the instructions may warn you that your score will be "corrected" for guessing. That is, a penalty will be applied. The incorrect answers will be deducted from the correct ones, or some other penalty formula will be used.

9) Review your answers

If you finish before time is called, go back to the questions you guessed or omitted to give them further thought. Review other answers if you have time.

10) Return your test materials

If you are ready to leave before others have finished or time is called, take ALL your materials to the monitor and leave quietly. Never take any test material with you. The monitor can discover whose papers are not complete, and taking a test booklet may be grounds for disqualification.

VIII. EXAMINATION TECHNIQUES

1) Read the general instructions carefully. These are usually printed on the first page of the exam booklet. As a rule, these instructions refer to the timing of the examination; the fact that you should not start work until the signal and must stop work at a signal, etc. If there are any *special* instructions, such as a choice of questions to be answered, make sure that you note this instruction carefully.

2) When you are ready to start work on the examination, that is as soon as the signal has been given, read the instructions to each question booklet, underline any key words or phrases, such as *least, best, outline, describe* and the like. In this way you will tend to answer as requested rather than discover on reviewing your paper that you *listed without describing*, that you selected the *worst* choice rather than the *best* choice, etc.

3) If the examination is of the objective or multiple-choice type – that is, each question will also give a series of possible answers: A, B, C or D, and you are called upon to select the best answer and write the letter next to that answer on your answer paper – it is advisable to start answering each question in turn. There may be anywhere from 50 to 100 such questions in the three or four hours allotted and you can see how much time would be taken if you read through all the questions before beginning to answer any. Furthermore, if you come across a question or group of questions which you know would be difficult to answer, it would undoubtedly affect your handling of all the other questions.

4) If the examination is of the essay type and contains but a few questions, it is a moot point as to whether you should read all the questions before starting to answer any one. Of course, if you are given a choice – say five out of seven and the like – then it is essential to read all the questions so you can eliminate the two that are most difficult. If, however, you are asked to answer all the questions, there may be danger in trying to answer the easiest one first because you may find that you will spend too much time on it. The best technique is to answer the first question, then proceed to the second, etc.

5) Time your answers. Before the exam begins, write down the time it started, then add the time allowed for the examination and write down the time it must be completed, then divide the time available somewhat as follows:
    - If 3-1/2 hours are allowed, that would be 210 minutes. If you have 80 objective-type questions, that would be an average of 2-1/2 minutes per question. Allow yourself no more than 2 minutes per question, or a total of 160 minutes, which will permit about 50 minutes to review.
    - If for the time allotment of 210 minutes there are 7 essay questions to answer, that would average about 30 minutes a question. Give yourself only 25 minutes per question so that you have about 35 minutes to review.

6) The most important instruction is to *read each question* and make sure you know what is wanted. The second most important instruction is to *time yourself properly* so that you answer every question. The third most important instruction is to *answer every question*. Guess if you have to but include something for each question. Remember that you will receive no credit for a blank and will probably receive some credit if you write something in answer to an essay question. If you guess a letter – say "B" for a multiple-choice question – you may have guessed right. If you leave a blank as an answer to a multiple-choice question, the examiners may respect your feelings but it will not add a point to your score. Some exams may penalize you for wrong answers, so in such cases *only*, you may not want to guess unless you have some basis for your answer.

7) Suggestions
    a. Objective-type questions
        1. Examine the question booklet for proper sequence of pages and questions
        2. Read all instructions carefully
        3. Skip any question which seems too difficult; return to it after all other questions have been answered
        4. Apportion your time properly; do not spend too much time on any single question or group of questions

5. Note and underline key words – *all, most, fewest, least, best, worst, same, opposite*, etc.
6. Pay particular attention to negatives
7. Note unusual option, e.g., unduly long, short, complex, different or similar in content to the body of the question
8. Observe the use of "hedging" words – *probably, may, most likely*, etc.
9. Make sure that your answer is put next to the same number as the question
10. Do not second-guess unless you have good reason to believe the second answer is definitely more correct
11. Cross out original answer if you decide another answer is more accurate; do not erase until you are ready to hand your paper in
12. Answer all questions; guess unless instructed otherwise
13. Leave time for review

   b. Essay questions
1. Read each question carefully
2. Determine exactly what is wanted. Underline key words or phrases.
3. Decide on outline or paragraph answer
4. Include many different points and elements unless asked to develop any one or two points or elements
5. Show impartiality by giving pros and cons unless directed to select one side only
6. Make and write down any assumptions you find necessary to answer the questions
7. Watch your English, grammar, punctuation and choice of words
8. Time your answers; don't crowd material

8) Answering the essay question

Most essay questions can be answered by framing the specific response around several key words or ideas. Here are a few such key words or ideas:

M's: manpower, materials, methods, money, management
P's: purpose, program, policy, plan, procedure, practice, problems, pitfalls, personnel, public relations

   a. Six basic steps in handling problems:
1. Preliminary plan and background development
2. Collect information, data and facts
3. Analyze and interpret information, data and facts
4. Analyze and develop solutions as well as make recommendations
5. Prepare report and sell recommendations
6. Install recommendations and follow up effectiveness

   b. Pitfalls to avoid
1. *Taking things for granted* – A statement of the situation does not necessarily imply that each of the elements is necessarily true; for example, a complaint may be invalid and biased so that all that can be taken for granted is that a complaint has been registered

2. *Considering only one side of a situation* – Wherever possible, indicate several alternatives and then point out the reasons you selected the best one
3. *Failing to indicate follow up* – Whenever your answer indicates action on your part, make certain that you will take proper follow-up action to see how successful your recommendations, procedures or actions turn out to be
4. *Taking too long in answering any single question* – Remember to time your answers properly

IX. AFTER THE TEST

Scoring procedures differ in detail among civil service jurisdictions although the general principles are the same. Whether the papers are hand-scored or graded by machine we have described, they are nearly always graded by number. That is, the person who marks the paper knows only the number – never the name – of the applicant. Not until all the papers have been graded will they be matched with names. If other tests, such as training and experience or oral interview ratings have been given, scores will be combined. Different parts of the examination usually have different weights. For example, the written test might count 60 percent of the final grade, and a rating of training and experience 40 percent. In many jurisdictions, veterans will have a certain number of points added to their grades.

After the final grade has been determined, the names are placed in grade order and an eligible list is established. There are various methods for resolving ties between those who get the same final grade – probably the most common is to place first the name of the person whose application was received first. Job offers are made from the eligible list in the order the names appear on it. You will be notified of your grade and your rank as soon as all these computations have been made. This will be done as rapidly as possible.

People who are found to meet the requirements in the announcement are called "eligibles." Their names are put on a list of eligible candidates. An eligible's chances of getting a job depend on how high he stands on this list and how fast agencies are filling jobs from the list.

When a job is to be filled from a list of eligibles, the agency asks for the names of people on the list of eligibles for that job. When the civil service commission receives this request, it sends to the agency the names of the three people highest on this list. Or, if the job to be filled has specialized requirements, the office sends the agency the names of the top three persons who meet these requirements from the general list.

The appointing officer makes a choice from among the three people whose names were sent to him. If the selected person accepts the appointment, the names of the others are put back on the list to be considered for future openings.

That is the rule in hiring from all kinds of eligible lists, whether they are for typist, carpenter, chemist, or something else. For every vacancy, the appointing officer has his choice of any one of the top three eligibles on the list. This explains why the person whose name is on top of the list sometimes does not get an appointment when some of the persons lower on the list do. If the appointing officer chooses the second or third eligible, the No. 1 eligible does not get a job at once, but stays on the list until he is appointed or the list is terminated.

X. HOW TO PASS THE INTERVIEW TEST

The examination for which you applied requires an oral interview test. You have already taken the written test and you are now being called for the interview test – the final part of the formal examination.

You may think that it is not possible to prepare for an interview test and that there are no procedures to follow during an interview. Our purpose is to point out some things you can do in advance that will help you and some good rules to follow and pitfalls to avoid while you are being interviewed.

What is an interview supposed to test?

The written examination is designed to test the technical knowledge and competence of the candidate; the oral is designed to evaluate intangible qualities, not readily measured otherwise, and to establish a list showing the relative fitness of each candidate – as measured against his competitors – for the position sought. Scoring is not on the basis of "right" and "wrong," but on a sliding scale of values ranging from "not passable" to "outstanding." As a matter of fact, it is possible to achieve a relatively low score without a single "incorrect" answer because of evident weakness in the qualities being measured.

Occasionally, an examination may consist entirely of an oral test – either an individual or a group oral. In such cases, information is sought concerning the technical knowledges and abilities of the candidate, since there has been no written examination for this purpose. More commonly, however, an oral test is used to supplement a written examination.

Who conducts interviews?

The composition of oral boards varies among different jurisdictions. In nearly all, a representative of the personnel department serves as chairman. One of the members of the board may be a representative of the department in which the candidate would work. In some cases, "outside experts" are used, and, frequently, a businessman or some other representative of the general public is asked to serve. Labor and management or other special groups may be represented. The aim is to secure the services of experts in the appropriate field.

However the board is composed, it is a good idea (and not at all improper or unethical) to ascertain in advance of the interview who the members are and what groups they represent. When you are introduced to them, you will have some idea of their backgrounds and interests, and at least you will not stutter and stammer over their names.

What should be done before the interview?

While knowledge about the board members is useful and takes some of the surprise element out of the interview, there is other preparation which is more substantive. It *is* possible to prepare for an oral interview – in several ways:

1) Keep a copy of your application and review it carefully before the interview

This may be the only document before the oral board, and the starting point of the interview. Know what education and experience you have listed there, and the sequence and dates of all of it. Sometimes the board will ask you to review the highlights of your experience for them; you should not have to hem and haw doing it.

2) Study the class specification and the examination announcement

Usually, the oral board has one or both of these to guide them. The qualities, characteristics or knowledges required by the position sought are stated in these documents. They offer valuable clues as to the nature of the oral interview. For example, if the job involves supervisory responsibilities, the announcement will usually indicate that knowledge of modern supervisory methods and the qualifications of the candidate as a supervisor will be tested. If so, you can expect such questions, frequently in the form of a hypothetical situation which you are expected to solve. NEVER go into an oral without knowledge of the duties and responsibilities of the job you seek.

3) Think through each qualification required

Try to visualize the kind of questions you would ask if you were a board member. How well could you answer them? Try especially to appraise your own knowledge and background in each area, *measured against the job sought*, and identify any areas in which you are weak. Be critical and realistic – do not flatter yourself.

4) Do some general reading in areas in which you feel you may be weak

For example, if the job involves supervision and your past experience has NOT, some general reading in supervisory methods and practices, particularly in the field of human relations, might be useful. Do NOT study agency procedures or detailed manuals. The oral board will be testing your understanding and capacity, not your memory.

5) Get a good night's sleep and watch your general health and mental attitude

You will want a clear head at the interview. Take care of a cold or any other minor ailment, and of course, no hangovers.

What should be done on the day of the interview?

Now comes the day of the interview itself. Give yourself plenty of time to get there. Plan to arrive somewhat ahead of the scheduled time, particularly if your appointment is in the fore part of the day. If a previous candidate fails to appear, the board might be ready for you a bit early. By early afternoon an oral board is almost invariably behind schedule if there are many candidates, and you may have to wait. Take along a book or magazine to read, or your application to review, but leave any extraneous material in the waiting room when you go in for your interview. In any event, relax and compose yourself.

The matter of dress is important. The board is forming impressions about you – from your experience, your manners, your attitude, and your appearance. Give your personal appearance careful attention. Dress your best, but not your flashiest. Choose conservative, appropriate clothing, and be sure it is immaculate. This is a business interview, and your appearance should indicate that you regard it as such. Besides, being well groomed and properly dressed will help boost your confidence.

Sooner or later, someone will call your name and escort you into the interview room. *This is it.* From here on you are on your own. It is too late for any more preparation. But remember, you asked for this opportunity to prove your fitness, and you are here because your request was granted.

What happens when you go in?

The usual sequence of events will be as follows: The clerk (who is often the board stenographer) will introduce you to the chairman of the oral board, who will introduce you to the other members of the board. Acknowledge the introductions before you sit down. Do not be surprised if you find a microphone facing you or a stenotypist sitting by. Oral interviews are usually recorded in the event of an appeal or other review.

Usually the chairman of the board will open the interview by reviewing the highlights of your education and work experience from your application – primarily for the benefit of the other members of the board, as well as to get the material into the record. Do not interrupt or comment unless there is an error or significant misinterpretation; if that is the case, do not hesitate. But do not quibble about insignificant matters. Also, he will usually ask you some question about your education, experience or your present job – partly to get you to start talking and to establish the interviewing "rapport." He may start the actual questioning, or turn it over to one of the other members. Frequently, each member undertakes the questioning on a particular area, one in which he is perhaps most competent, so you can expect each member to participate in the examination. Because time is limited, you may also expect some rather abrupt switches in the direction the questioning takes, so do not be upset by it. Normally, a board member will not pursue a single line of questioning unless he discovers a particular strength or weakness.

After each member has participated, the chairman will usually ask whether any member has any further questions, then will ask you if you have anything you wish to add. Unless you are expecting this question, it may floor you. Worse, it may start you off on an extended, extemporaneous speech. The board is not usually seeking more information. The question is principally to offer you a last opportunity to present further qualifications or to indicate that you have nothing to add. So, if you feel that a significant qualification or characteristic has been overlooked, it is proper to point it out in a sentence or so. Do not compliment the board on the thoroughness of their examination – they have been sketchy, and you know it. If you wish, merely say, "No thank you, I have nothing further to add." This is a point where you can "talk yourself out" of a good impression or fail to present an important bit of information. Remember, *you close the interview yourself.*

The chairman will then say, "That is all, Mr. _____, thank you." Do not be startled; the interview is over, and quicker than you think. Thank him, gather your belongings and take your leave. Save your sigh of relief for the other side of the door.

How to put your best foot forward

Throughout this entire process, you may feel that the board individually and collectively is trying to pierce your defenses, seek out your hidden weaknesses and embarrass and confuse you. Actually, this is not true. They are obliged to make an appraisal of your qualifications for the job you are seeking, and they want to see you in your best light. Remember, they must interview all candidates and a non-cooperative candidate may become a failure in spite of their best efforts to bring out his qualifications. Here are 15 suggestions that will help you:

1) Be natural – Keep your attitude confident, not cocky

If you are not confident that you can do the job, do not expect the board to be. Do not apologize for your weaknesses, try to bring out your strong points. The board is interested in a positive, not negative, presentation. Cockiness will antagonize any board member and make him wonder if you are covering up a weakness by a false show of strength.

2) Get comfortable, but don't lounge or sprawl

Sit erectly but not stiffly. A careless posture may lead the board to conclude that you are careless in other things, or at least that you are not impressed by the importance of the occasion. Either conclusion is natural, even if incorrect. Do not fuss with your clothing, a pencil or an ashtray. Your hands may occasionally be useful to emphasize a point; do not let them become a point of distraction.

3) Do not wisecrack or make small talk

This is a serious situation, and your attitude should show that you consider it as such. Further, the time of the board is limited – they do not want to waste it, and neither should you.

4) Do not exaggerate your experience or abilities

In the first place, from information in the application or other interviews and sources, the board may know more about you than you think. Secondly, you probably will not get away with it. An experienced board is rather adept at spotting such a situation, so do not take the chance.

5) If you know a board member, do not make a point of it, yet do not hide it

Certainly you are not fooling him, and probably not the other members of the board. Do not try to take advantage of your acquaintanceship – it will probably do you little good.

6) Do not dominate the interview

Let the board do that. They will give you the clues – do not assume that you have to do all the talking. Realize that the board has a number of questions to ask you, and do not try to take up all the interview time by showing off your extensive knowledge of the answer to the first one.

7) Be attentive

You only have 20 minutes or so, and you should keep your attention at its sharpest throughout. When a member is addressing a problem or question to you, give him your undivided attention. Address your reply principally to him, but do not exclude the other board members.

8) Do not interrupt

A board member may be stating a problem for you to analyze. He will ask you a question when the time comes. Let him state the problem, and wait for the question.

9) Make sure you understand the question

Do not try to answer until you are sure what the question is. If it is not clear, restate it in your own words or ask the board member to clarify it for you. However, do not haggle about minor elements.

10) Reply promptly but not hastily

A common entry on oral board rating sheets is "candidate responded readily," or "candidate hesitated in replies." Respond as promptly and quickly as you can, but do not jump to a hasty, ill-considered answer.

11) Do not be peremptory in your answers

A brief answer is proper – but do not fire your answer back. That is a losing game from your point of view. The board member can probably ask questions much faster than you can answer them.

12) Do not try to create the answer you think the board member wants

He is interested in what kind of mind you have and how it works – not in playing games. Furthermore, he can usually spot this practice and will actually grade you down on it.

13) Do not switch sides in your reply merely to agree with a board member

Frequently, a member will take a contrary position merely to draw you out and to see if you are willing and able to defend your point of view. Do not start a debate, yet do not surrender a good position. If a position is worth taking, it is worth defending.

14) Do not be afraid to admit an error in judgment if you are shown to be wrong

The board knows that you are forced to reply without any opportunity for careful consideration. Your answer may be demonstrably wrong. If so, admit it and get on with the interview.

15) Do not dwell at length on your present job

The opening question may relate to your present assignment. Answer the question but do not go into an extended discussion. You are being examined for a *new* job, not your present one. As a matter of fact, try to phrase ALL your answers in terms of the job for which you are being examined.

Basis of Rating

Probably you will forget most of these "do's" and "don'ts" when you walk into the oral interview room. Even remembering them all will not ensure you a passing grade. Perhaps you did not have the qualifications in the first place. But remembering them will help you to put your best foot forward, without treading on the toes of the board members.

Rumor and popular opinion to the contrary notwithstanding, an oral board wants you to make the best appearance possible. They know you are under pressure – but they also want to see how you respond to it as a guide to what your reaction would be under the pressures of the job you seek. They will be influenced by the degree of poise you display, the personal traits you show and the manner in which you respond.

ABOUT THIS BOOK

This book contains tests divided into Examination Sections. Go through each test, answering every question in the margin. We have also attached a sample answer sheet at the back of the book that can be removed and used. At the end of each test look at the answer key and check your answers. On the ones you got wrong, look at the right answer choice and learn. Do not fill in the answers first. Do not memorize the questions and answers, but understand the answer and principles involved. On your test, the questions will likely be different from the samples. Questions are changed and new ones added. If you understand these past questions you should have success with any changes that arise. Tests may consist of several types of questions. We have additional books on each subject should more study be advisable or necessary for you. Finally, the more you study, the better prepared you will be. This book is intended to be the last thing you study before you walk into the examination room. Prior study of relevant texts is also recommended. NLC publishes some of these in our Fundamental Series. Knowledge and good sense are important factors in passing your exam. Good luck also helps. So now study this Passbook, absorb the material contained within and take that knowledge into the examination. Then do your best to pass that exam.

EXAMINATION SECTION

SAMPLE QUESTIONS
BIOGRAPHICAL INVENTORY

The questions included in the Biographical Inventory ask for information about you and your background. These kinds of questions are often asked during an oral interview. For years, employers have been using interviews to relate personal history, preferences, and attitudes to job success. This Biographical Inventory attempts to do the same and includes questions which have been shown to be related to job success. It has been found that successful employees tend to select some answers more often than other answers, while less successful employees tend to select different answers. The questions in the Biographical Inventory do not have a single correct answer. Every choice is given some credit. More credit is given for answers selected more often by successful employees.

These Biographical Inventory questions are presented for illustrative purposes only. The answers have not been linked to the answers of successful employees; therefore, we cannot designate any "correct" answer(s).

DIRECTIONS: You may only mark ONE response to each question. It is possible that none of the answers applies well to you. However, one of the answers will surely be true (or less inaccurate) for you than others. In such a case, mark that answer. <u>Answer each question honestly.</u> The credit that is assigned to each response on the actual test is based upon how successful employees described themselves when honestly responding to the questions. *PRINT THE LETTER OF THE CORRECT ANSWER IN THE SPACE AT THE RIGHT.*

1. Generally, in your work assignments, would you prefer
   A. to work on one thing at a time
   B. to work on a couple of things at a time
   C. to work on many things at the same time

   1.____

2. In the course of a week, which of the following gives you the GREATEST satisfaction?
   A. Being told you have done a good job.
   B. Helping other people to solve their problems.
   C. Coming up with a new or unique way to handle a situation.
   D. Having free time to devote to personal interests.

   2.____

EXAMINATION SECTION

TEST 1

DIRECTIONS: Each question or incomplete statement is followed by several suggested answers or completions. Select the one that BEST answers the question or completes the statement. *PRINT THE LETTER OF THE CORRECT ANSWER IN THE SPACE AT THE RIGHT.*

1. While a senior in high school, I was absent
    A. never
    B. seldom
    C. frequently
    D. more than 10 days
    E. only when I felt bored

   1._____

2. While in high school, I failed classes
    A. never
    B. once
    C. twice
    D. more than twice
    E. at least four times

   2._____

3. During class discussions in my high school classes, I usually
    A. listened without participating
    B. participated as much as possible
    C. listened until I had something to add to the discussion
    D. disagreed with others simply for the sake of argument
    E. laughed at stupid ideas

   3._____

4. My high school grade point average (on a 4.0 scale) was
    A. 2.0 or lower
    B. 2.1 to 2.5
    C. 2.6 to 3.0
    D. 3.1 to 3.5
    E. 3.6 to 4.0

   4._____

5. As a high school student, I completed my assignments
    A. as close to the due date as I could manage
    B. whenever the teacher gave me an extension
    C. frequently
    D. on time
    E. when they were interesting

   5._____

6. While in high school, I participated in
    A. athletic and non-athletic extracurricular activities
    B. athletic extracurricular activities
    C. non-athletic extracurricular activities
    D. no extracurricular activities
    E. mandatory afterschool programs

   6._____

7. In high school, I made the honor roll
   A. several times
   B. once
   C. more than once
   D. twice
   E. I cannot remember

8. Upon graduation from high school, I received _____ honors.
   A. academic and non-academic
   B. academic
   C. non-academic
   D. no
   E. I cannot remember

9. While attending high school, I worked at a paid job or as a volunteer
   A. never
   B. every so often
   C. 5 to 10 hours a month
   D. more than 10 hours a month
   E. more than 15 hours a month

10. During my senior year of high school, I skipped school
    A. whenever I could
    B. once a week
    C. several times a week
    D. not at all
    E. when I got bored

11. I was suspended from high school
    A. not at all
    B. once or twice
    C. once or twice, for fighting
    D. several times
    E. more times than I can remember

12. During high school, my fellow students and teachers considered me
    A. above average
    B. below average
    C. average
    D. underachieving
    E. underachieving and prone to fighting

13. An effective leader is someone who
    A. inspires confidence in his/her followers
    B. inspires fear in his/her followers
    C. tells subordinates exactly what they should do
    D. creates an environment in which subordinates feel insecure about their job security and performance
    E. makes as few decisions as possible

14. While a student, I spent my summers and holiday breaks 14._____
    A. in summer or remedial classes
    B. traveling
    C. working
    D. relaxing
    E. spending time with my friends

15. As a high school student, I cut classes 15._____
    A. frequently
    B. when I didn't like them
    C. sometimes
    D. rarely
    E. when I needed the sleep

16. In high school, I received academic honors 16._____
    A. not at all
    B. once
    C. twice
    D. several times
    E. I cannot remember

17. As a student, I failed _____ classes. 17._____
    A. no
    B. two
    C. three
    D. four
    E. more than four

18. Friends describe me as 18._____
    A. introverted
    B. hot-tempered
    C. unpredictable
    D. quiet
    E. easygoing

19. During my high school classes, I preferred to 19._____
    A. remain silent during discussions
    B. do other homework during discussions
    C. participate frequently in discussions
    D. argue with others as much as possible
    E. laugh at the stupid opinions of others

20. As a high school student, I was placed on academic probation 20._____
    A. not at all
    B. once
    C. twice
    D. three times
    E. more than three times

21. At work, being a team player means to   21._____
    A. compromise your ideals and beliefs
    B. compensate for the incompetence of others
    C. count on others to compensate for your inexperience
    D. cooperate with others to get a project finished
    E. rely on others to get the job done

22. My friends from school remember me primarily as a(n)   22._____
    A. person who loved to party
    B. ambitious student
    C. athlete
    D. joker
    E. fighter

23. My school experience is memorable primarily because of   23._____
    A. the friends I made
    B. the sorority/fraternity I was able to join
    C. the social activities I participated in
    D. my academic achievements
    E. the money I spent

24. A friend who is applying for a job asks you to help him pass the   24._____
    mandatory drug test by substituting your urine sample for his. You should
    A. help him by supplying the sample
    B. supply the sample and insist he seek drug counseling
    C. supply the sample, but tell him that this is the only time you'll help
       in this way
    D. call the police
    E. refuse

25. As a student, I handed in my assignments when   25._____
    A. they were due
    B. I could get an extension
    C. they were interesting
    D. my friends reminded me to
    E. I was able to

KEY (CORRECT ANSWERS)

1. A	11. A	21. D
2. A	12. A	22. B
3. C	13. A	23. D
4. E	14. C	24. E
5. D	15. D	25. A
6. A	16. D	
7. A	17. A	
8. A	18. E	
9. E	19. C	
10. D	20. A	

TEST 2

DIRECTIONS: Each question or incomplete statement is followed by several suggested answers or completions. Select the one that BEST answers the question or completes the statement. *PRINT THE LETTER OF THE CORRECT ANSWER IN THE SPACE AT THE RIGHT.*

1. At work you are accused of a minor infraction which you did not commit. Your first reaction is to
    A. call a lawyer
    B. speak to your supervisor about the mistake
    C. call the police
    D. yell at the person who did commit the infraction
    E. accept the consequences regardless of your guilt or innocence

    1._____

2. As a student, I began to prepare for final exams
    A. the night before taking them
    B. when the professor handed out the review sheets
    C. several weeks before taking them
    D. when my friends began to prepare for their exams
    E. the morning of the exam

    2._____

3. At work, I am known as
    A. popular
    B. quiet
    C. intense
    D. easygoing
    E. dedicated

    3._____

4. The most important quality in a coworker is
    A. friendliness
    B. cleanliness
    C. good sense of humor
    D. dependability
    E. good listening skills

    4._____

5. In the past year, I have stayed home from work
    A. frequently
    B. only when I felt depressed
    C. rarely
    D. only when I felt overwhelmed
    E. only to run important errands

    5._____

6. For me, the best thing about school was the
    A. chance to strengthen my friendships and develop new ones
    B. chance to test my abilities and develop new ones
    C. number of extracurricular activities and clubs
    D. chance to socialize
    E. chance to try several different majors

    6._____

7. As an employee, my weakest skill is
    A. controlling my temper
    B. organizational ability
    C. ability to effectively understand directions
    D. ability to effectively manage others
    E. ability to communicate my thoughts in writing

    7._____

8. As an employee, my greatest strength would be
    A. my sense of loyalty
    B. organizational ability
    C. punctuality
    D. dedication
    E. ability to intimidate others

    8._____

9. If asked by my company to learn a new job-related skill, my reaction would be to
    A. ask for a raise
    B. ask for overtime pay
    C. question the necessity of the skill
    D. cooperate with some reluctance
    E. cooperate with enthusiasm

    9._____

10. When I disagree with others, I tend to
    A. listen quietly despite my disagreement
    B. laugh openly at the person I disagree with
    C. ask the person to explain their views before I respond
    D. leave the conversation before my anger gets the best of me
    E. point out exactly why the person is wrong

    10._____

11. When I find myself in a situation which is confusing or unclear, my reaction is to
    A. pretend I am not confused
    B. remain calm and, if necessary, ask someone else for clarification
    C. grow frustrated and angry
    D. walk away from the situation
    E. immediately insist that someone explain things to me

    11._____

12. If you were placed in a supervisory position, which of the following abilities would you consider to be most important to your job performance?
    A. Stubbornness
    B. The ability to hear all sides of a story before making a decision
    C. Kindness
    D. The ability to make and stick to a decision
    E. Patience

    12._____

13. What is your highest level of education?
    A. Less than a high school diploma
    B. High school diploma or equivalency
    C. Graduate of community college
    D. Graduate of a four-year accredited college
    E. Degree from graduate school

    13._____

14. When asked to supervise other workers, your approach should be to   14._____
    A. ask for management wages since you're doing management work
    B. give the workers direction and supervise every aspect of the process
    C. give the workers direction and then allow them to do the job
    D. hand the workers their job specifications
    E. do the work yourself, since you're uncomfortable supervising others

15. Which of the following best describes you?   15._____
    A. Need little or no supervision
    B. Resent too much supervision
    C. Require as much supervision as my peers
    D. Require slightly more supervision than my peers
    E. Require close supervision

16. You accept a job which requires an ability to perform several tasks at once. What is the best way to handle such a position?   16._____
    A. With strong organizational skills and close attention to detail
    B. By delegating the work to someone with strong organizational skills
    C. Staying focused on one task at a time, no matter what happens
    D. Working on one task at a time until each task is successfully completed
    E. Asking your supervisor to help you

17. Which of the following best describes your behavior when you disagree with someone? You   17._____
    A. state your own point of view as quickly and loudly as you can
    B. listen quietly and keep your opinions to yourself
    C. listen to the other person's perspective and then carefully point out all the flaws in their logic
    D. list all of the ignorant people who agree with the opposing point of view
    E. listen to the other person's perspective and then explain your own perspective

18. As a new employee, you make several mistakes during your first week of work. You react by   18._____
    A. learning from your mistakes and moving on
    B. resigning
    C. blaming it on your supervisor
    D. refusing to talk about it
    E. blaming yourself

19. My ability to communicate effectively with others is   19._____
    A. below average
    B. average
    C. above average
    D. far above average
    E. far below average

20. In which of the following areas are you most highly skilled? 20._____
    A. Written communication
    B. Oral communication
    C. Ability to think quickly in difficult situations
    D. Ability to work with a broad diversity of people and personalities
    E. Organizational skills

21. As a worker, you are assigned to work with a partner whom you dislike. 21._____
    You should
    A. immediately report the problem to your supervisor
    B. ask your partner not to speak to you during working hours
    C. tell your colleagues about your differences
    D. tell your partner why you dislike him/her
    E. work with your partner regardless of your personal feelings

22. During high school, what was your most common afterschool activity? 22._____
    A. Remaining after school to participate in various clubs and
       organizations (band, sports, etc.)
    B. Making up for missed classes
    C. Punishment or detention
    D. Going straight to an afterschool job
    E. Spending the afternoon at home or with friends

23. During high school, in which of the following subjects did you receive the 23._____
    highest grades?
    A. English, history, social studies
    B. Math, science
    C. Vocational classes
    D. My grades were consistent in all subjects
    E. Classes I liked

24. When faced with an overwhelming number of duties at work, your 24._____
    reaction is to
    A. do all of the work yourself, no matter what the cost
    B. delegate some responsibilities to capable colleagues
    C. immediately ask your supervisor for help
    D. put off as much work as possible until you can get to it
    E. take some time off to relax and clear your mind

25. Which of the following best describes your desk at your current or most 25._____
    recent job?
    A. Messy and disorganized
    B. Neat and organized
    C. Messy but organized
    D. Neat but disorganized
    E. Messy

KEY (CORRECT ANSWERS)

1. B
2. C
3. E
4. D
5. C

6. B
7. E
8. D
9. E
10. C

11. B
12. D
13. E
14. C
15. A

16. A
17. E
18. A
19. C
20. C

21. E
22. A
23. D
24. B
25. B

TEST 3

DIRECTIONS: Each question or incomplete statement is followed by several suggested answers or completions. Select the one that BEST answers the question or completes the statement. *PRINT THE LETTER OF THE CORRECT ANSWER IN THE SPACE AT THE RIGHT.*

1. When asked to take on extra responsibility at work, in order to help out a coworker who is overwhelmed, your response is to
    A. ask for overtime pay
    B. complain to your supervisor that you are being taken advantage of
    C. help the coworker to the best of your ability
    D. ask the coworker to come back some other time
    E. give the coworker some advice on how to get his/her job done

1._____

2. At my last job, I was promoted
    A. not at all
    B. once
    C. twice
    D. three times
    E. more than three times

2._____

3. You are faced with an overwhelming deadline at work. Your reaction is to
    A. procrastinate until the last minute
    B. procrastinate until someone notices that you need some help
    C. notify your supervisor that you cannot complete the work on your own
    D. work in silence without asking any questions
    E. arrange your schedule so that you can get the work done before the deadline

3._____

4. When you feel yourself under deadline pressure at work, your response is
    A. make sure you keep to a schedule which allows you to complete the work on time
    B. wait until just before the deadline to complete the work
    C. ask someone else to do the work
    D. grow so obsessive about the work that your coworkers feel compelled to help you
    E. ask your supervisor immediately for help

4._____

5. Which of the following best describes your appearance at your current or most recent position?
    A. Well-groomed, neat and clean
    B. Unkempt, but dressed neatly
    C. Messy and dirty clothing
    D. Unshaven and untidy
    E. Clean-shaven, but sloppily dressed

5._____

6. Which of the following best describes the way you react to making a difficult decision?
	A. Consult with the people you're closest to before making the decision
	B. Make the decision entirely on your own
	C. Consult only with those people whom your decision will affect
	D. Consult with everyone you know, in an effort to make a decision that will please everyone
	E. Forget about the decision until you have to make it

6._____

7. If placed in a supervisory role, which of the following characteristics would you rely on most heavily when dealing with the employees you supervise?
	A. Kindness
	B. Cheeriness
	C. Honesty
	D. Hostility
	E. Aloofness

7._____

8. When confronted with gossip at work, your typical reaction is to
	A. participate
	B. listen without participating
	C. notify your supervisor
	D. excuse yourself from the discussion
	E. confront your coworkers about their problem

8._____

9. In the past two years, how many jobs have you held?
	A. None
	B. One
	C. Two
	D. Three
	E. More than three

9._____

10. In your current or most recent job, your favorite part of the job is the part which involves
	A. telling other people what they're doing wrong
	B. supervising others
	C. working without supervision to finish a project
	D. written communication
	E. oral communication

10._____

11. Your supervisor asks you about a colleague who is applying for a position which you also want. You react by
	A. commenting honestly on the colleague's work performance
	B. enhancing the person's negative traits
	C. informing your supervisor about your colleague's personal problems
	D. telling your supervisor that you would be better in the position
	E. refusing to comment

11._____

12. Which of these best describes your responsibilities in your last job?   12._____
    A. Entirely supervisory
    B. Much supervisory responsibility
    C. Equal amounts of supervisory and non-supervisory responsibility
    D. Some supervisory responsibilities
    E. No supervisory responsibilities

13. How much written communication did your previous or most recent job   13._____
    require of you?
    A. A great deal
    B. Some
    C. I don't remember
    D. A small amount
    E. None

14. In the past two years, how many times have you been fired from a job?   14._____
    A. None
    B. Once
    C. Twice
    D. Three times
    E. More than three times

15. How many hours per week have you spent working for volunteer   15._____
    organizations in the past year?
    A. 10 to 20
    B. 5 to 10
    C. 3 to 5
    D. 1 to 3
    E. None

16. Your efforts at volunteer work usually revolve around which of the   16._____
    following types of organizations?
    A. Religious
    B. Community-based organization working to improve the community
    C. Charity on behalf of the poor
    D. Charity on behalf of the infirm or handicapped
    E. Other

17. Which of the following best describes your professional history?   17._____
    Promoted at _____ coworkers.
    A. a much faster rate than
    B. a slightly faster rate than
    C. the same rate as
    D. a slightly slower rate than
    E. a much slower rate than

18. Which of the following qualities do you most appreciate in a coworker?   18._____
    A. Friendliness
    B. Dependability
    C. Good looks
    D. Silence
    E. Forgiveness

19. When you disagree with a supervisor's instructions or opinion about how to complete a project, your reaction is to
    A. inform your supervisor that you refuse to complete the project according to his or her instructions
    B. inform your colleagues of your supervisor's incompetence
    C. accept your supervisor's instructions in silence
    D. voice your concerns and then complete the project according to your own instincts
    E. voice your concerns and then complete the project according to your supervisor's instructions

19._____

20. Which of the following best describes your reaction to close supervision and specific direction from your supervisors? You
    A. listen carefully to the direction, then figure out a way to do the job more effectively
    B. complete the job according to the given specifications
    C. show some initiative by doing the job your way
    D. ask someone else to do the job for you
    E. listen carefully to the directions, and then figure out a better way to do the job which will save more money

20._____

21. At work, you are faced with a difficult decision. You react by
    A. seeking advice from your colleagues
    B. following your own path regardless of the consequences
    C. asking your supervisor what you should do
    D. keeping the difficulties to yourself
    E. working for a solution which will please everyone

21._____

22. If asked to work with a person whom you dislike, your response would be
    A. to ask your supervisor to allow you to work with someone else
    B. to ask your coworker to transfer to another department or project
    C. talk to your coworker about the proper way to behave at work
    D. pretend the coworker is your best friend for the sake of your job
    E. set aside your personal differences in order to complete the job

22._____

23. As a supervisor, which of the following incentives would you use to motivate your employees?
    A. Fear of losing their jobs
    B. Fear of their supervisors
    C. Allowing employees to provide their input on a number of policies
    D. Encouraging employees to file secret reports regarding colleagues' transgressions
    E. All of the above

23._____

24. A fellow worker, with whom you enjoy a close friendship, has a substance abuse problem which has gone undetected. You suspect the problem may be affecting his job. You would
    A. ask the worker if the problem is affecting his job performance
    B. warn the worker that he must seek counseling or you will report him
    C. wait a few weeks to see whether the worker's problem really is affecting his job
    D. discuss it with your supervisor
    E. wait for the supervisor to discover the problem

24._____

25. In the past two months, you have missed work
    A. never
    B. once
    C. twice
    D. three times
    E. more than three times

25._____

KEY (CORRECT ANSWERS)

1. C	11. A	21. A
2. C	12. D	22. E
3. E	13. B	23. C
4. A	14. A	24. D
5. A	15. C	25. A
6. A	16. B	
7. C	17. A	
8. D	18. B	
9. B	19. E	
10. C	20. B	

EXAMINATION SECTION
TEST 1

DIRECTIONS: Each question or incomplete statement is followed by several suggested answers or completions. Select the one that BEST answers the question or completes the statement. *PRINT THE LETTER OF THE CORRECT ANSWER IN THE SPACE AT THE RIGHT.*

1. Good procedure in handling complaints from the public may be divided into the following four principal stages:
   I. Investigation of the complaint
   II. Receipt of the complaint
   III. Assignment of responsibility for investigation and correction
   IV. Notification of correction

   The ORDER in which these stages ordinarily come is:
   A. III, II, I, IV   B. II, III, I, IV   C. II, III, IV, I   D. II, IV, III, I

   1.____

2. The department may expect the MOST severe public criticism if
   A. it asks for an increase in its annual budget
   B. it purchases new and costly street cleaning equipment
   C. sanitation officers and men are reclassified to higher salary grades
   D. there is delay in cleaning streets of snow

   2.____

3. The MOST important function of public relations in the department should be to
   A. develop cooperation on the part of the public in keeping streets clean
   B. get stricter penalties enacted for health code violations
   C. recruit candidates for entrance positions who ca be developed into supervisors
   D. train career personnel so that they can advance in the department

   3.____

4. The one of the following which has MOST frequently elicited unfavorable public comment has been
   A. dirty sidewalks or streets   B. dumping on lot
   C. failure to curb dogs   D. overflowing garbage cans

   4.____

5. It has been suggested that, as a public relations measure, sections hold *open house* for the public.
   The MOST effective time for this would be
   A. during the summer when children are not in school and can accompany their parents
   B. during the winter when show is likely to fall and the public can see snow removal preparations
   C. immediately after a heavy snow storm when department snow removal operations are in full progress
   D. when street sanitation is receiving general attention as during *Keep City Clean* week

   5.____

6. When a public agency conducts a public relations program, it is MOST likely to find that each recipient of its message will
   A. disagree with the basic purpose of the message if the officials are not well known to him
   B. accept the message if it is presented by someone perceived as having a definite intention to persuade
   C. ignore the message unless it is presented in a literate and clever manner
   D. give greater attention to certain portions of the message as a result of his individual and cultural differences

7. Following are three statements about public relations and communications:
   I. A person who seeks to influence public opinion can speed up a trend
   II. Mass communications is the exposure of a mass audience to an idea
   III. All media are equally effective in reaching opinion leaders
   Which of the following choices CORRECTLY classifies the above statements into those which are correct and those which are not?
   A. I and II are correct, but III is not.
   B. II and III are correct, but I is not.
   C. I and III are correct, but II is not.
   D. III is correct, but I and II are not.

8. Public relations experts say that MAXIMUM effect for a message results from
   A. concentrating in one medium
   B. ignoring mass media and concentrating on *opinion makers*
   C. presenting only those factors which support a given position
   D. using a combination of two or more of the available media

9. To assure credibility and avoid hostility, the public relations man MUST
   A. make certain his message is truthful, not evasive or exaggerated
   B. make sure his message contains some dire consequence if ignored
   C. repeat the message often enough so that it cannot be ignored
   D. try to reach as many people and groups as possible

10. The public relations man MUST be prepared to assume that members of his audience
    A. may have developed attitudes toward his proposals—favorable, neutral, or unfavorable
    B. will be immediately hostile
    C. will consider his proposals with an open mind
    D. will invariably need an introduction to his subject

11. The one of the following statements that is CORRECT is:
    A. When a stupid question is asked of you by the public, it should be disregarded
    B. If you insist on formality between you and the public, the public will not be able to ask stupid questions that cannot be answered
    C. The public should be treated courteously, regardless of how stupid their questions may be
    D. You should explain to the public how stupid their questions are

12. With regard to public relations, the MOST important item which should be emphasized in an employee training program is that
    A. each inspector is a public relations agent
    B. an inspector should give the public all the information it asks for
    C. it is better to make mistakes and give erroneous information than to tell the public that you do not know the correct answer to their problem
    D. public relations is so specialized a field that only persons specially trained in it should consider it

12.____

13. Members of the public frequently ask about departmental procedures.
    Of the following, it is BEST to
    A. advise the public to put the question in writing so that he can get a proper formal reply
    B. refuse to answer because this is a confidential matter
    C. explain the procedure as briefly as possible
    D. attempt to avoid the issue by discussing other matters

13.____

14. The effectiveness of a public relations program in a public agency such as the authority is BEST indicated by the
    A. amount of mass media publicity favorable to the policies of the authority
    B. morale of those employees who directly serve the patrons of the authority
    C. public's understanding and support of the authority's program and policies
    D. number of complaint received by the authority from patrons using its facilities

14.____

15. In an attempt to improve public opinion about a certain idea, the BEST course of action for an agency to take would be to present the
    A. clearest statements of the idea even though the language is somewhat technical
    B. idea as the result of long-term studies
    C. idea in association with something familiar to most people
    D. idea as the viewpoint of the majority leaders

15.____

16. The fundamental factor in any agency's community relations program is
    A. an outline of the objectives
    B. relations with the media
    C. the everyday actions of the employees
    D. a well-planned supervisory program

16.____

17. The FUNDAMENTAL factor in the success of a community relations program is
    A. true commitment by the community
    B. true commitment by the administration
    C. a well-planned, systematic approach
    D. the actions of individuals in their contacts with the public

17.____

18. The statement below which is LEAST correct is:
    A. Because of selection standards, the supervisor frequently encounters problems resulting from subordinates' inability to express themselves in the language of the profession.
    B. Distortion of the meaning of a communication is usually brought about by a failure to use language that has a precise meaning to others.
    C. The term *filtering* is the distortion or dilution of content of a communication that occurs as information is passed from individual to individual.
    D. The complexity of the *communications net* will directly affect.

19. Consider the following three statements that may or may not be CORRECT:
    I. In order to prevent the stifling of communications flow, supervisors should insist that employees use the formal communications network.
    II. Two-way communications are faster and more accurate than one-way communications.
    III. There is a direct correlation between the effectiveness of communications and the total setting in which they occur.
    The choice below which MOST accurately describes the above statement is:
    A. All three are correct.
    B. All three are incorrect.
    C. More than one statement is correct.
    D. Only one of the statements is correct.

20. The statement below which is MOST inaccurate is:
    A. The supervisor's most important tool in learning whether or not he is communicating well is feedback.
    B. Follow-up is essential if useful feedback is to be obtained.
    C. Subordinates are entitled, as a matter of right, to explanations from management concerning the reasons for orders or directives.
    D. A skilled supervisor is often able to use the grapevine to good advantage.

21. *Since concurrence by those affected is not sought, this kind of communication can be issued with relative ease.*
    The kind of communication being referred to in this quotation is
    A. autocratic   B. democratic   C. directive   D. free-rein

22. The statement below which is LEAST correct is:
    A. Clarity is more important in oral communicating than in written since the readers of a written communication can read it over again.
    B. Excessive use of abbreviations in written communications should be avoided.
    C. Short sentences with simple words are preferred over complex sentences and difficult words in a written communication.
    D. The *newspaper* style of writing ordinarily simplifies expression and facilitates understanding.

23. Which one of the following is the MOST important factor for the department to consider in building a good public image?
    A. A good working relationship with the news media
    B. An efficient community relations program
    C. An efficient system for handling citizen complaints
    D. The proper maintenance of facilities and equipment
    E. The behavior of individuals in their contacts with the public.

23.____

24. It has been said that the ability to communicate clearly and concisely is the MOST important single skill of the supervisor.
    Consider the following statements:
    I. The adage, *Actions speak louder than words*, has NO application in superior/subordinate communications since good communications are accomplished with words.
    II. The environment in which a communication takes place will *rarely* determine its effect.
    III. Words are symbolic representations which must be associated with past experience or else they are meaningless.
    The choice below which MOST accurately describes the above statements is:
    A. I, II, and III are correct.
    B. I and II are correct, but III is not.
    C. I and III are correct, but II is not.
    D. III is correct, but I and II are not.
    E. I, II, and III are incorrect.

24.____

25. According to expert opinion, the effectiveness of an organization is very dependent upon good upward, downward, and lateral communications. Lateral communications are most important to the activity of coordinating the efforts of organizational units. Before real communication can take place at any level, barriers to communication must be recognized, understood, and removed.
    Consider the following three statements:
    I. The *principal* barrier to good communications is a failure to establish empathy between sender and receiver.
    II. The difference in status or rank between the sender and receiver of a communication may be a communications barrier.
    III. Communications are easier if they travel upward from subordinate to superior
    The choice below which MOST accurately describes the above statements is:
    A. I, II and III are incorrect.   B. I and II are incorrect.
    C. I, II, and III are correct.   D. I and II are correct.
    E. I and III are incorrect.

25.____

KEY (CORRECT ANSWERS)

1.	B	11.	C
2.	D	12.	A
3.	A	13.	C
4.	A	14.	C
5.	D	15.	C
6.	D	16.	C
7.	A	17.	D
8.	D	18.	A
9.	A	19.	D
10.	A	20.	C

21.	A
22.	A
23.	E
24.	D
25.	E

EXAMINATION SECTION
TEST 1

For each of the following items, circle the answer that best reflects the accuracy of the given statement, according to your own values, opinions, and experience.

1. In most situations, I value cooperation over competition.

   A. Very Accurate
   B. Moderately Accurate
   C. Neither Accurate nor Inaccurate
   D. Moderately Inaccurate
   E. Very Inaccurate

2. In work or in school, I've tried to do more than what's expected of me.

   A. Very Accurate
   B. Moderately Accurate
   C. Neither Accurate nor Inaccurate
   D. Moderately Inaccurate
   E. Very Inaccurate

3. Most of my problems are caused by other people.

   A. Very Accurate
   B. Moderately Accurate
   C. Neither Accurate nor Inaccurate
   D. Moderately Inaccurate
   E. Very Inaccurate

4. It's reasonable to say that a person's race is in some way related to the likelihood that he or she will commit a crime.

   A. Very Accurate
   B. Moderately Accurate
   C. Neither Accurate nor Inaccurate
   D. Moderately Inaccurate
   E. Very Inaccurate

5. My respect for a person's authority relies entirely on my respect for them as an individual, and has nothing to do with his or her official position.

   A. Very Accurate
   B. Moderately Accurate
   C. Neither Accurate nor Inaccurate
   D. Moderately Inaccurate
   E. Very Inaccurate

6. When I was in school, I never cheated on a test or assignment.

   A. Very Accurate
   B. Moderately Accurate
   C. Neither Accurate nor Inaccurate
   D. Moderately Inaccurate
   E. Very Inaccurate

7. I feel comfortable around most people, even if they're strangers.

   A. Very Accurate
   B. Moderately Accurate
   C. Neither Accurate nor Inaccurate
   D. Moderately Inaccurate
   E. Very Inaccurate

8. It's acceptable for an employee to borrow property from the workplace if the person who takes it intends to return it when he or she is finished with it.

   A. Very Accurate
   B. Moderately Accurate
   C. Neither Accurate nor Inaccurate
   D. Moderately Inaccurate
   E. Very Inaccurate

9. If it's clear that a person is not likely to receive adequate punishment for a crime or infraction, it's only fair to inflict some form of discipline on that person to make up for any likely lapses injustice.

    A. Very Accurate
    B. Moderately Accurate
    C. Neither Accurate nor Inaccurate
    D. Moderately Inaccurate
    E. Very Inaccurate

10. In previous work experience, I have been reluctant or unable to take on extra work or overtime on short notice.

    A. Very Accurate
    B. Moderately Accurate
    C. Neither Accurate nor Inaccurate
    D. Moderately Inaccurate
    E. Very Inaccurate

11. The casual use of illegal substances, if it's done only recreationally and on weekends, has no effect on a person's performance on the job during the work week.

    A. Very Accurate
    B. Moderately Accurate
    C. Neither Accurate nor Inaccurate
    D. Moderately Inaccurate
    E. Very Inaccurate

12. I am sometimes overwhelmed by events.

    A. Very Accurate
    B. Moderately Accurate
    C. Neither Accurate nor Inaccurate
    D. Moderately Inaccurate
    E. Very Inaccurate

13. If I don't agree with a certain rule, I see nothing wrong with breaking it, as long as it doesn't hurt anyone else.

    A. Very Accurate
    B. Moderately Accurate
    C. Neither Accurate nor Inaccurate
    D. Moderately Inaccurate
    E. Very Inaccurate

14. I get angry easily.

    A. Very Accurate
    B. Moderately Accurate
    C. Neither Accurate nor Inaccurate
    D. Moderately Inaccurate
    E. Very Inaccurate

15. As long as an employee finishes all his work on time at the end of the day, there's nothing wrong with coming back from lunch late.

    A. Very Accurate
    B. Moderately Accurate
    C. Neither Accurate nor Inaccurate
    D. Moderately Inaccurate
    E. Very Inaccurate

16. I enjoy beginning new things.

    A. Very Accurate
    B. Moderately Accurate
    C. Neither Accurate nor Inaccurate
    D. Moderately Inaccurate
    E. Very Inaccurate

17. When I have a number of tasks to be done, I prioritize them and tackle them immediately in order of importance.

    A. Very Accurate
    B. Moderately Accurate
    C. Neither Accurate nor Inaccurate
    D. Moderately Inaccurate
    E. Very Inaccurate

18. I would have no reservations about working for a supervisor who is of a different race or gender than I am.

    A. Very Accurate
    B. Moderately Accurate
    C. Neither Accurate nor Inaccurate
    D. Moderately Inaccurate
    E. Very Inaccurate

19. I'd rather help other people to do better than punish them for doing wrong.

    A. Very Accurate
    B. Moderately Accurate
    C. Neither Accurate nor Inaccurate
    D. Moderately Inaccurate
    E. Very Inaccurate

20. In the past, I've had personality clashes with fellow students or co-workers whom I disliked or with whom I disagreed.

    A. Very Accurate
    B. Moderately Accurate
    C. Neither Accurate nor Inaccurate
    D. Moderately Inaccurate
    E. Very Inaccurate

21. Confrontations are usually unpleasant, but sometimes necessary.

    A. Very Accurate
    B. Moderately Accurate
    C. Neither Accurate nor Inaccurate
    D. Moderately Inaccurate
    E. Very Inaccurate

22. I generally believe that other people have good intentions.

    A. Very Accurate
    B. Moderately Accurate
    C. Neither Accurate nor Inaccurate
    D. Moderately Inaccurate
    E. Very Inaccurate

23. When I have a lot of information to sort through, I have difficulty making up my mind.

    A. Very Accurate
    B. Moderately Accurate
    C. Neither Accurate nor Inaccurate
    D. Moderately Inaccurate
    E. Very Inaccurate

24. In tense situations, I choose my words with care.

    A. Very Accurate
    B. Moderately Accurate
    C. Neither Accurate nor Inaccurate
    D. Moderately Inaccurate
    E. Very Inaccurate

25. A person who works through his or her lunch break should automatically be able to go home early.

    A. Very Accurate   B. Moderately Accurate
    C. Neither Accurate nor Inaccurate   D. Moderately Inaccurate
    E. Very Inaccurate

Experiences and Traits

For each of the 25 items, score your response according to the list below. Then add the scores of all 25 items to arrive at a single number.

1. A=4;B=3;C=2;D=1;E=0
2. A=4;B=3;C=2;D=1;E=0
3. A=0;B=1;C=2;D=3;E=4
4. A=0;B=1;C=2;D=3;E=4
5. A=0;B=1;C=2;D=3;E=4

6. A=4;B=3;C=2;D=1;E=0
7. A=4;B=3;C=2;D=1;E=0
8. A=0;B=1;C=2;D=3;E=4
9. A=0;B=1;C=2;D=3;E=4
10. A=0;B=1;C=2;D=3;E=4

11. A=0;B=1;C=2;D=3;E=4
12. A=0;B=1;C=2;D=3;E=4
13. A=0;B=1;C=2;D=3;E=4
14. A=0;B=1;C=2;D=3;E=4
15. A=0;B=1;C=2;D=3;E=4

16. A=4;B=3;C=2;D=1;E=0
17. A=4;B=3;C=2;D=1;E=0
18. A=4;B=3;C=2;D=1;E=0
19. A=4;B=3;C=2;D=1;E=0
20. A=0;B=1;C=2;D=3;E=4

21. A=4;B=3;C=2;D=1;E=0
22. A=4;B=3;C=2;D=1;E=0
23. A=0;B=1;C=2;D=3;E=4
24. A=4;B=3;C=2;D=1;E=0
25. A=0;B=1;C=2;D=3;E=4

The following scores serve as an approximate guide to your compatibility with a career in law enforcement but should not be taken as the final word.

    85-100 points   Most compatible
    70-84 points   Compatible
    50-69 points   Somewhat compatible
    0-49 points   Incompatible

TEST 2

For each of the following items, circle the answer that best reflects the accuracy of the given statement, according to your own values, opinions, and experience.

1. I find it difficult to approach people I don't know well.

    A. Very Accurate
    C. Neither Accurate nor Inaccurate
    E. Very Inaccurate
    B. Moderately Accurate
    D. Moderately Inaccurate

2. I'm not really interested in hearing about other people's problems.

    A. Very Accurate
    C. Neither Accurate nor Inaccurate
    E. Very Inaccurate
    B. Moderately Accurate
    D. Moderately Inaccurate

3. Sometimes I don't know why I do the things I do.

    A. Very Accurate
    C. Neither Accurate nor Inaccurate
    E. Very Inaccurate
    B. Moderately Accurate
    D. Moderately Inaccurate

4. I am hesitant to take charge of a group that has no clear leadership.

    A. Very Accurate
    C. Neither Accurate nor Inaccurate
    E. Very Inaccurate
    B. Moderately Accurate
    D. Moderately Inaccurate

5. I enjoy examining myself and the direction my life is taking.

    A. Very Accurate
    C. Neither Accurate nor Inaccurate
    E. Very Inaccurate
    B. Moderately Accurate
    D. Moderately Inaccurate

6. I believe there is no absolute right or wrong.

    A. Very Accurate
    C. Neither Accurate nor Inaccurate
    E. Very Inaccurate
    B. Moderately Accurate
    D. Moderately Inaccurate

7. I always pay my bills on time.

    A. Very Accurate
    C. Neither Accurate nor Inaccurate
    E. Very Inaccurate
    B. Moderately Accurate
    D. Moderately Inaccurate

8. In this world it's difficult to be both honest and successful.

    A. Very Accurate
    C. Neither Accurate nor Inaccurate
    E. Very Inaccurate
    B. Moderately Accurate
    D. Moderately Inaccurate

9. I am intimidated by strong personalities.

    A. Very Accurate
    B. Moderately Accurate
    C. Neither Accurate nor Inaccurate
    D. Moderately Inaccurate
    E. Very Inaccurate

10. In past work experience, I was unable to find value in work that wasn't personally rewarding to me.

    A. Very Accurate
    B. Moderately Accurate
    C. Neither Accurate nor Inaccurate
    D. Moderately Inaccurate
    E. Very Inaccurate

11. I often do things I later regret.

    A. Very Accurate
    B. Moderately Accurate
    C. Neither Accurate nor Inaccurate
    D. Moderately Inaccurate
    E. Very Inaccurate

12. I feel sympathy for those who are worse off than I am.

    A. Very Accurate
    B. Moderately Accurate
    C. Neither Accurate nor Inaccurate
    D. Moderately Inaccurate
    E. Very Inaccurate

13. If a rule gets in the way of my doing my job well, I'll look for ways around it.

    A. Very Accurate
    B. Moderately Accurate
    C. Neither Accurate nor Inaccurate
    D. Moderately Inaccurate
    E. Very Inaccurate

14. I think a person's dress and appearance are important in the work environment.

    A. Very Accurate
    B. Moderately Accurate
    C. Neither Accurate nor Inaccurate
    D. Moderately Inaccurate
    E. Very Inaccurate

15. There have been times when my own personal use of drugs or alcohol has adversely affected my job performance.

    A. Very Accurate
    B. Moderately Accurate
    C. Neither Accurate nor Inaccurate
    D. Moderately Inaccurate
    E. Very Inaccurate

16. In past work or school experience, I have never been in a position to supervise the work of others.

    A. Very Accurate
    B. Moderately Accurate
    C. Neither Accurate nor Inaccurate
    D. Moderately Inaccurate
    E. Very Inaccurate

17. If I need to, I can talk other people into doing what I think is necessary.

    A. Very Accurate
    B. Moderately Accurate
    C. Neither Accurate nor Inaccurate
    D. Moderately Inaccurate
    E. Very Inaccurate

18. I usually prefer order to chaos.

    A. Very Accurate
    B. Moderately Accurate
    C. Neither Accurate nor Inaccurate
    D. Moderately Inaccurate
    E. Very Inaccurate

19. When I'm faced with an ethical dilemma, I listen to my conscience.

    A. Very Accurate
    B. Moderately Accurate
    C. Neither Accurate nor Inaccurate
    D. Moderately Inaccurate
    E. Very Inaccurate

20. When I communicate with other people, I can easily sense their emotional state.

    A. Very Accurate
    B. Moderately Accurate
    C. Neither Accurate nor Inaccurate
    D. Moderately Inaccurate
    E. Very Inaccurate

21. I set high standards for myself and others.

    A. Very Accurate
    B. Moderately Accurate
    C. Neither Accurate nor Inaccurate
    D. Moderately Inaccurate
    E. Very Inaccurate

22. In school or at work, I am never late.

    A. Very Accurate
    B. Moderately Accurate
    C. Neither Accurate nor Inaccurate
    D. Moderately Inaccurate
    E. Very Inaccurate

23. I sometimes make assumptions about people based on their racial or ethnic backgrounds.

    A. Very Accurate
    B. Moderately Accurate
    C. Neither Accurate nor Inaccurate
    D. Moderately Inaccurate
    E. Very Inaccurate

24. I tend to focus on the positive aspects of a complex situation, rather than the negatives.

    A. Very Accurate
    B. Moderately Accurate
    C. Neither Accurate nor Inaccurate
    D. Moderately Inaccurate
    E. Very Inaccurate

25. I can manage several tasks at the same time.

    A. Very Accurate
    B. Moderately Accurate
    C. Neither Accurate nor Inaccurate
    D. Moderately Inaccurate
    E. Very Inaccurate

Experiences and Traits

For each of the 25 items, score your response according to the list below. Then add the scores of all 25 items to arrive at a single number.

1. A=0;B=1;C=2;D=3;E=4
2. A=0;B=1;C=2;D=3;E=4
3. A=0;B=1;C=2;D=3;E=4
4. A=0;B=1;C=2;D=3;E=4
5. A=4;B=3;C=2;D=1;E=0

6. A=0;B=1;C=2;D=3;E=4
7. A=4;B=3;C=2;D=1;E=0
8. A=0;B=1;C=2;D=3;E=4
9. A=0;B=1;C=2;D=3;E=4
10. A=0;B=1;C=2;D=3;E=4

11. A=0;B=1;C=2;D=3;E=4
12. A=4;B=3;C=2;D=1;E=0
13. A=0;B=1;C=2;D=3;E=4
14. A=4;B=3;C=2;D=1;E=0
15. A=0;B=1;C=2;D=3;E=4

16. A=0;B=1;C=2;D=3;E=4
17. A=4;B=3;C=2;D=1;E=0
18. A=4;B=3;C=2;D=1;E=0
19. A=4;B=3;C=2;D=1;E=0
20. A=4;B=3;C=2;D=1;E=0

21. A=4;B=3;C=2;D=1;E=0
22. A=4;B=3;C=2;D=1;E=0
23. A=0;B=1;C=2;D=3;E=4
24. A=4;B=3;C=2;D=1;E=0
25. A=4;B=3;C=2;D=1;E=0

The following scores serve as an approximate guide to your compatibility with a career in law enforcementbut should not be taken as the final word.

85-100 points	Most compatible
70-84 points	Compatible
50-69 points	Somewhat compatible
0-49 points	Incompatible

SAMPLE CLERK-CARRIER TEST

Now that you have studied the instructions and taken the practice tests in this book, you are ready to take the Sample Tests. There is one Sample Test for Clerk-Carrier.

The Sample Tests are exactly like the ones you will have to take in the examinations. The time allowances and the numbers of questions are the same as they are in the real tests.

At the back of the book you will find some answer sheets to use. These answer sheets are like the ones you will use in the examinations.

When you are ready to try a Sample Test, tear out an answer sheet from the back of the book. Then do what the instructions tell you to do. Remember that in the address-checking and memory for addresses sections you will lose credit for wrong answers. In the address-checking section it will be better not to guess.

After you have finished answering the questions for a sample test, compare your answers with the correct answers for that test and see how well you did.

Clerk-Carrier Test

Time Required for Each Part
- Part A
    - Samples — 3 minutes
    - Test — 6 minutes
- Part B
    - Samples and Study — 6 minutes (Approximately)
    - Test—List 1 Practice — 3 minutes
    - Test—List 2 Practice — 3 minutes
    - Study — 5 minutes
    - Test—List 1 — 5 minutes
    - Test—List 2 — 5 minutes
- Part C
    - Samples — 3 minutes
    - Test — 30 minutes
- Part D
    - Samples — 20 minutes (Approximately)
    - Test — 30 minutes

INTERPRETATION OF TEST SCORES ON SAMPLE CLERK-CARRIER TEST

After you have taken a Part of the test or after you have finished the test, compare your answers with those given in the Correct Answers to Sample Test. You will find them on page **20**.

For the Address Checking (Part A), count the number that you got right and the number that you got wrong. (If you didn't mark anything for a question, it doesn't get counted.)

From the number right
Subtract the number wrong
This number (the difference) is your score⟶

The meaning of the score is as follows:

52 or higher	Good.
Between 32 and 51	Fair.
Below 32	You need more practice.

Go back and see where you made your mistakes. Were you careless? Did you work too slowly?

In the Memory for Addresses (Part B), only Test-List 2, which you recorded on your answer sheet, counts. For that Part, count the number that you got right and the number that you got wrong. (If you didn't mark anything for a question, it doesn't get counted.)

Divide the number wrong by 4. _____
From the number right
Subtract ¼ the number wrong
This number (the difference) is your score⟶

The meaning of the score is as follows:

44 or higher	Good.
Between 26 and 43	Fair.
Below 26	You need more practice.

Go back and see where you made your mistakes. Were you careless? Did you work too slowly? Try to find out what is the best way for you to memorize.

For Word Meaning and Reading, your score is the number right: _____.

The meaning of the score is as follows:

24 or higher	Good.
Between 20 and 23	Fair.
Below 20	You need more study.

Go back and see where you made your mistakes. Were you careless? Did you spend too much time on the questions that were hard for you? Were there words that you didn't know? If you didn't know the words, try to build up your vocabulary. Some ways of doing this are suggested on page 58.

For Number Series (Part D), your score is the number right: _____.

The meaning of the score is as follows:

17 or higher	Good.
Between 12 and 16	Fair.
Below 12	You need more practice.

Go back and see why you didn't get a higher score. Did you make arithmetic mistakes? Were you careless? Did you have trouble finding the rule? If you did, keep working with the questions until you find the rules. See the suggestions **given**. Sometimes it helps to leave a question that is bothering you and go on and work on the others. Then come back to the ones you had to leave.

In the Clerk-Carrier test your scores on vocabulary, reading, and number series will be added together in order to get your score on the general abilities section of the test.

SAMPLE CLERK-CARRIER TEST

There are four parts to this test. It is best to have a friend to watch the time for you. The correct time limit for each part is given on page 1. Be careful not to take any more time than given in the instructions for each part.

Tear out an answer sheet from the back of the book and use it to mark your answers for each part of this test.

Directions and Samples for Part A

In this Part you will be given addresses to compare. On your answer sheet darken the box under A if the two addresses are exactly *Alike* in every way. Darken the box under D if they are *Different*.

Here are some sample questions for you to do. Mark your answers to them on the Sample Answer Sheet on this page. You should not take more than *3 minutes* to read and study the material on this page of the test.

Show your answer to a question by darkening completely the box corresponding to the letter that is the same as the letter of your answer. You must keep your mark within the box. If you have to erase a mark, be sure to erase it completely. Mark only one answer for each question.

1 ... 2134 S 20th St   2134 S 20th St
    Since the two addresses are exactly alike, mark A for question 1 on the Sample Answer Sheet.
2 ... 4608 N Warnock St   4806 N Warnock St
3 ... 1202 W Girard Dr   1202 W Girard Rd
4 ... Chappaqua N Y 10514   Chappaqua N Y 10514
5 ... 2207 Markland Ave   2207 Markham Ave

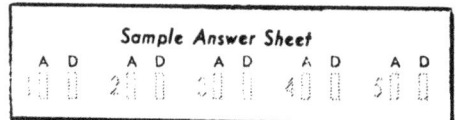

Now compare your answers with the Correct Answers to Sample Questions. If your answers are not the same as the correct answers shown, go back and study the samples to see where you made a mistake.

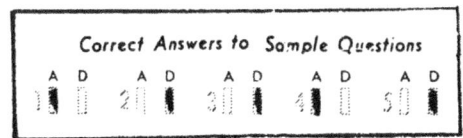

It will be to your advantage to work as quickly and accurately as possible since your score on this part of the test will be based on the number of wrong answers as well as the number of right answers. It is not expected that you will be able to finish all the questions in the time allowed.

Be sure to use a pencil so that you can make erasures.

Look at your answer sheet. The answers to this part of the examination must be marked in Part A of the answer sheet. Notice also that the answer spaces are numbered across the page. Mark the answer for question 1 in space 1.

When you begin the test, work as fast as you can without making mistakes. Do as many questions as you can in the time allowed.

You will have *6 minutes* to answer as many of the 95 questions as you can.

DO NOT TURN THIS PAGE UNTIL YOU ARE READY TO BEGIN THE TEST.

PART A

REMEMBER: Mark your answers on the separate answer sheet. Use "A" for "Alike" and "D" for "Different." Work as quickly as you can.

1 ...	405 Winter Rd NW	405 Winter Rd NW
2 ...	607 S Calaveras Rd	607 S Calaveras Rd
3 ...	8406 La Casa St	8406 La Cosa St
4 ...	121 N Rippon St	121 N Rippon St
5 ...	Wideman Ark	Wiseman Ark
6 ...	Sodus NY 14551	Sodus NY 14551
7 ...	3429 Hermosa Dr	3429 Hermoso Dr
8 ...	3628 S Zeeland St	3268 S Zeeland St
9 ...	1330 Cheverly Ave NE	1330 Cheverly Ave NE
10 ...	1689 N Derwood Dr	1689 N Derwood Dr
11 ...	3886 Sunrise Ct	3886 Sunrise Ct
12 ...	635 La Calle Mayor	653 La Calle Mayor
13 ...	2560 Lansford Pl	2560 Lansford St
14 ...	4631 Central Ave	4631 Central Ave
15 ...	Mason City Iowa 50401	Mason City Iowa 50401
16 ...	758 Los Arboles Ave SE	758 Los Arboles Ave SW
17 ...	3282 E Downington St	3282 E Dunnington St
18 ...	7117 N Burlingham Ave	7117 N Burlingham Ave
19 ...	32 Oaklawn Blvd	32 Oakland Blvd
20 ...	1274 Manzana Rd	1274 Manzana Rd
21 ...	4598 E Kenilworth Dr	4598 E Kenilworth Dr
22 ...	Dayton Okla 73449	Dagton Okla 73449
23 ...	1172 W 83rd Ave	1127 W 83rd Ave
24 ...	6434 E Pulaski St	6434 E Pulaski Ct
25 ...	2764 N Rutherford Pl	2764 N Rutherford Pl
26 ...	565 Greenville Blvd SE	565 Greenview Blvd SE
27 ...	Washington D C 20013	Washington D C 20018
28 ...	3824 Massasoit St	3824 Massasoit St
29 ...	22 Sagnaw Pkwy	22 Saganaw Pkwy
30 ...	Byram Conn 10573	Byram Conn 10573
31 ...	1928 S Fairfield Ave	1928 S Fairfield St
32 ...	36218 Overhills Dr	36218 Overhills Dr
33 ...	516 Avenida de Las Americas NW	516 Avenida de Las Americas NW
34 ...	7526 Naraganset Pl SW	7526 Naraganset Pl SW
35 ...	52626 W Ogelsby Dr	52626 W Ogelsby Dr
36 ...	1003 Winchester Rd	1003 Westchester Rd
37 ...	3478 W Cavanaugh Ct	3478 W Cavenaugh Ct
38 ...	Kendall Calif 90551	Kendell Calif 90551
39 ...	225 El Camino Blvd	225 El Camino Ave
40 ...	7310 Via de los Pisos	7310 Via de los Pinos
41 ...	1987 Wellington Ave SW	1987 Wellington Ave SW
42 ...	3124 S 71st St	3142 S 71st St
43 ...	729 Lincolnwood Blvd	729 Lincolnwood Blvd
44 ...	1166 N Beaumont Dr	1166 S Beaumont Dr
45 ...	3224 W Winecona Pl	3224 W Winecona Pl
46 ...	608 La Calle Bienvenida	607 La Calle Bienvenida
47 ...	La Molte Iowa 52045	La Molte Iowa 52045

GO ON TO NUMBER 48 ON THE NEXT PAGE.

48	8625 Armitage Ave NW	8625 Armitage Ave NW
49	2343 Broadview Ave	2334 Broadview Ave
50	4279 Sierra Grande Ave NE	4279 Sierra Grande Dr NE
51	165 32d Ave	165 32d Ave
52	12742 N Deerborn St	12724 N Deerborn St
53	114 Estancia Ave	141 Estancia Ave
54	351 S Berwyn Rd	351 S Berwyn Pl
55	7732 Avenida Manana SW	7732 Avenida Manana SW
56	6337 C St SW	6337 G St SW
57	57895 E Drexyl Ave	58795 E Drexyl Ave
58	Altro Tex 75923	Altra Tex 75923
59	3465 S Nashville St	3465 N Nashville St
60	1226 Odell Blvd NW	1226 Oddell Blvd NW
61	94002 Chappel Ct	94002 Chappel Ct
62	512 La Vega Dr	512 La Veta Dr
63	8774 W Winona Pl	8774 E Winona Pl
64	6431 Ingleside St SE	6431 Ingleside St SE
65	2270 N Leanington St	2270 N Leanington St
66	235 Calle de Los Vecinos	235 Calle de Los Vecinos
67	3987 E Westwood Ave	3987 W Westwood Ave
68	Skamokawa Wash	Skamohawa Wash
69	2674 E Champlain Cir	2764 E Champlain Cir
70	8751 Elmhurst Blvd	8751 Elmwood Blvd
71	6649 Solano Dr	6649 Solana Dr
72	4423 S Escenaba St	4423 S Escenaba St
73	1198 N St NW	1198 M St NW
74	Sparta Ga	Sparta Va
75	96753 Wrightwood Ave	96753 Wrightwood Ave
76	2445 Sangamow Ave SE	2445 Sangamow Ave SE
77	5117 E 67 Pl	5171 E 67 Pl
78	847 Mesa Grande Pl	847 Mesa Grande Ct
79	1100 Cermaken St	1100 Cermaker St
80	321 Tijeras Ave NW	321 Tijeras Ave NW
81	3405 Prospect St	3405 Prospect St
82	6643 Burlington Pl	6643 Burlingtown Pl
83	851 Esperanza Blvd	851 Esperanza Blvd
84	Jenkinjones W Va	Jenkinjones W Va
85	1008 Pennsylvania Ave SE	1008 Pennsylvania Ave SW
86	2924 26th St N	2929 26th St N
87	7115 Highland Dr	7115 Highland Dr
88	Chaptico Md	Chaptica Md
89	3508 Camron Mills Rd	3508 Camron Mills Rd
90	67158 Capston Dr	67158 Capston Dr
91	3613 S Taylor Ave	3631 S Taylor Ave
92	2421 Menokin Dr	2421 Menokin Dr
93	3226 M St NW	3226 N St NW
94	1201 S Court House Rd	1201 S Court House Rd
95	Findlay Ohio 45840	Findley Ohio 45840

STOP.

**If you finish before the time is up, check your answers for Part A.
Do not go to any other part.**

When the time is up, turn to page 6.

Samples for Part B

Part B has five boxes labeled A, B, C, D, and E. Each box contains five addresses. Three of the five addresses are groups of street addresses like 2100–2799 Mall, 4800–4999 Cliff and 1900–2299 Laurel, and two are names of places. They are different in each box. You will be given two lists of addresses. For each street address or name in the list, you are to decide in which lettered box (A, B, C, D, or E) it belongs and then mark that box on the answer sheet. For List 1, the boxes will be shown on the same page with the addresses. While you are working on List 2, you will not be able to look at the boxes. Then you will have to match the addresses with the correct box from memory. Try to memorize the location of as many addresses as you can.

A	B	C	D	E
2100–2799 Mall Ceres 4800–4999 Cliff Natoma 1900–2299 Laurel	3900–4399 Mall Cedar 4000–4299 Cliff Foster 2300–2999 Laurel	4400–4599 Mall Niles 3300–3999 Cliff Dexter 3200–3799 Laurel	3400–3899 Mall Cicero 4500–4799 Cliff Pearl 3000–3199 Laurel	2800–3399 Mall Delhi 4300–4499 Cliff Magnet 1500–1899 Laurel

Sample Questions:

1. 3300–3999 Cliff—This address is in box C. So you would darken box C.
2. Natoma—This name is in box A. So you would darken box A.
3. Foster
4. 1500–1899 Laurel
5. 3900–4399 Mall
6. Pearl
7. 3200–3799 Laurel

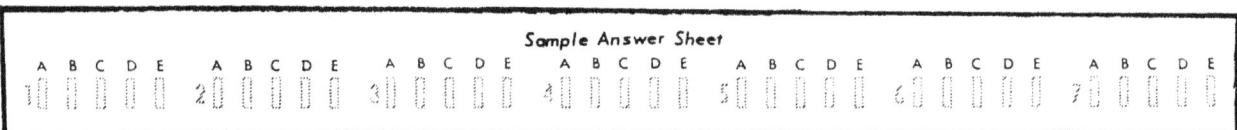

The answers to samples 3 to 7 are: 3B, 4E, 5B, 6D, and 7C.

In List 1 the boxes with the addresses will be before your eyes. Therefore you will be able to check your answers by looking at the top of the page. However, checking takes time and the more you remember, the faster you will be able to work. On List 2 the boxes with the addresses will *not* be shown. Then you will have only your memory to depend on when answering the questions. Thus, memory will be very important in this test.

Different people study in different ways. Many people find it easier to learn the addresses in one box at a time than to learn all the addresses at once.

You will now have *3 minutes* to study the addresses and letters so that you will have a good idea of the letter that goes with each address. Do not spend more than 3 minutes studying the addresses.

Now memorize the addresses in the boxes. These are the addresses that will be in the test. TRY TO LEARN THE LOCATION OF AS MANY ADDRESSES AS YOU CAN. Cover each box with your hand and see if you can repeat, to yourself, the addresses in that box.

DO NOT TURN THIS PAGE UNTIL THE TIME IS UP. THEN TURN TO PAGE 7.

PART B

List 1

For each question, mark the top answer sheet on the next page to show the letter of the box in which the address belongs. Try to remember the location of as many addresses as you can. You will now have *3 minutes* for List 1. If you are not sure of an answer you should guess.

A	B	C	D	E
2100–2799 Mall Ceres 4800–4999 Cliff Natoma 1900–2299 Laurel	3900–4399 Mall Cedar 4000–4299 Cliff Foster 2300–2999 Laurel	4400–4599 Mall Niles 3300–3999 Cliff Dexter 3200–3799 Laurel	3400–3899 Mall Cicero 4500–4799 Cliff Pearl 3000–3199 Laurel	2800–3399 Mall Delhi 4300–4499 Cliff Magnet 1500–1899 Laurel

1. Magnet
2. Niles
3. 3400–3899 Mall
4. 1900–2299 Laurel
5. Cicero
6. Dexter
7. 2300–2999 Laurel
8. 3300–3999 Cliff

9. 3200–3799 Laurel
10. 2100–2799 Mall
11. Pearl
12. 3200–3799 Laurel
13. Ceres
14. 4500–4799 Cliff
15. 3900–4399 Mall
16. Delhi

17. 4300–4499 Cliff
18. 3000–3199 Laurel
19. Ceres
20. Foster
21. Natoma
22. 4400–4599 Mall
23. Cedar
24. 2300–2999 Laurel

25. 1500–1899 Laurel
26. 4000–4299 Cliff
27. Dexter
28. Magnet
29. 3300–3999 Cliff
30. 3400–3899 Mall
31. Niles
32. 2100–2799 Mall

33. 1900–2299 Laurel
34. Cedar
35. Pearl
36. 2800–3399 Mall
37. 4800–4999 Cliff
38. 3900–4399 Mall
39. Foster
40. 3000–3199 Laurel

41. Ceres
42. Niles
43. 3400–3899 Mall
44. Delhi
45. 2300–2999 Laurel
46. 4500–4799 Cliff
47. Dexter
48. Magnet

49. 3300–3999 Cliff
50. Cicero
51. 4300–4499 Cliff
52. 3900–4399 Mall
53. Natoma
54. 3200–3799 Laurel
55. Pearl
56. 4000–4299 Cliff

57. 4500–4799 Cliff
58. 2100–2799 Mall
59. Foster
60. 4400–4599 Mall
61. 4800–4999 Cliff
62. Ceres
63. 2800–3399 Mall
64. 1500–1899 Laurel

65. Natoma
66. 3000–3199 Laurel
67. 4000–4299 Cliff
68. Niles
69. 2300–2999 Laurel
70. Magnet
71. Delhi
72. 4400–4599 Mall

73. Cicero
74. Cedar
75. 2800–3399 Mall
76. 1900–2299 Laurel
77. Dexter
78. Pearl
79. 4300–4499 Cliff
80. 3900–4399 Mall

81. Foster
82. 4800–4999 Cliff
83. Delhi
84. Ceres
85. 1500–1899 Laurel
86. Natoma
87. 2800–3399 Mall
88. Niles

STOP.

If you finish before the time is up, go back and check your answers for the questions on this page. Do not go to any other page until the time is up.

List 2

For each question, mark the answer sheet on the next page to show the letter of the box in which the address belongs. If you are not sure of an answer, you should guess. You will record your answers on the next page. While you are working on List 2, do not turn to any other page. You will have *3 minutes* to do this list.

1. Cedar
2. 4300–4499 Cliff
3. 4400–4599 Mall
4. Natoma
5. 2300–2999 Laurel
6. 4500–4799 Cliff
7. Ceres
8. 3400–3899 Mall

9. Delhi
10. Dexter
11. 1900–2299 Laurel
12. 3300–3999 Cliff
13. Cicero
14. 4000–4299 Cliff
15. 2100–2799 Mall
16. Foster

17. Magnet
18. Ceres
19. 2800–3399 Mall
20. 3200–3799 Laurel
21. 4300–4499 Cliff
22. Pearl
23. 3900–4399 Mall
24. Natoma

25. 4800–4999 Cliff
26. 1500–1899 Laurel
27. Cedar
28. 4400–4599 Mall
29. 4500–4799 Cliff
30. Dexter
31. 3000–3199 Laurel
32. Niles

33. Delhi
34. 3900–4399 Mall
35. Cicero
36. Dexter
37. 4800–4999 Cliff
38. 2300–2999 Laurel
39. 2100–2799 Mall
40. 3300–3999 Cliff

41. 3400–3899 Mall
42. 4300–4499 Cliff
43. Ceres
44. Foster
45. Magnet
46. 3200–3799 Laurel
47. Pearl
48. 1500–1899 Laurel

49. 4500–4799 Cliff
50. 1900–2299 Laurel
51. Niles
52. 3300–3999 Cliff
53. 2800–3399 Mall
54. Cicero
55. Delhi
56. 4000–4299 Cliff

57. Dexter
58. Magnet
59. 3000–3199 Laurel
60. 3900–4399 Mall
61. Natoma
62. 3000–3199 Laurel
63. 4300–4499 Cliff
64. Cedar

65. 4400–4599 Mall
66. 1500–1899 Laurel
67. 4800–4999 Cliff
68. Delhi
69. Pearl
70. 2300–2999 Laurel
71. 4500–4799 Cliff
72. Niles

73. 4000–4299 Cliff
74. 3400–3899 Mall
75. 1900–2299 Laurel
76. 2800–3399 Mall
77. Ceres
78. Magnet
79. Cicero
80. 3200–3799 Laurel

81. 3000–3199 Laurel
82. 3900–4399 Mall
83. Natoma
84. 3300–3999 Cliff
85. 3400–3899 Mall
86. Foster
87. 2100–2799 Mall
88. 4300–4499 Cliff

If you finish before the time is up, go back and check your answers to this part only. When the time is up turn back to page 6 and study the boxes again. You will have *5 minutes* to restudy the addresses. When that time is up, go on to page 7 and do that list again, using the bottom answer sheet on page 8. You will have *5 minutes* to do List 1 again. When that time is up turn to page 11 and read the instructions.

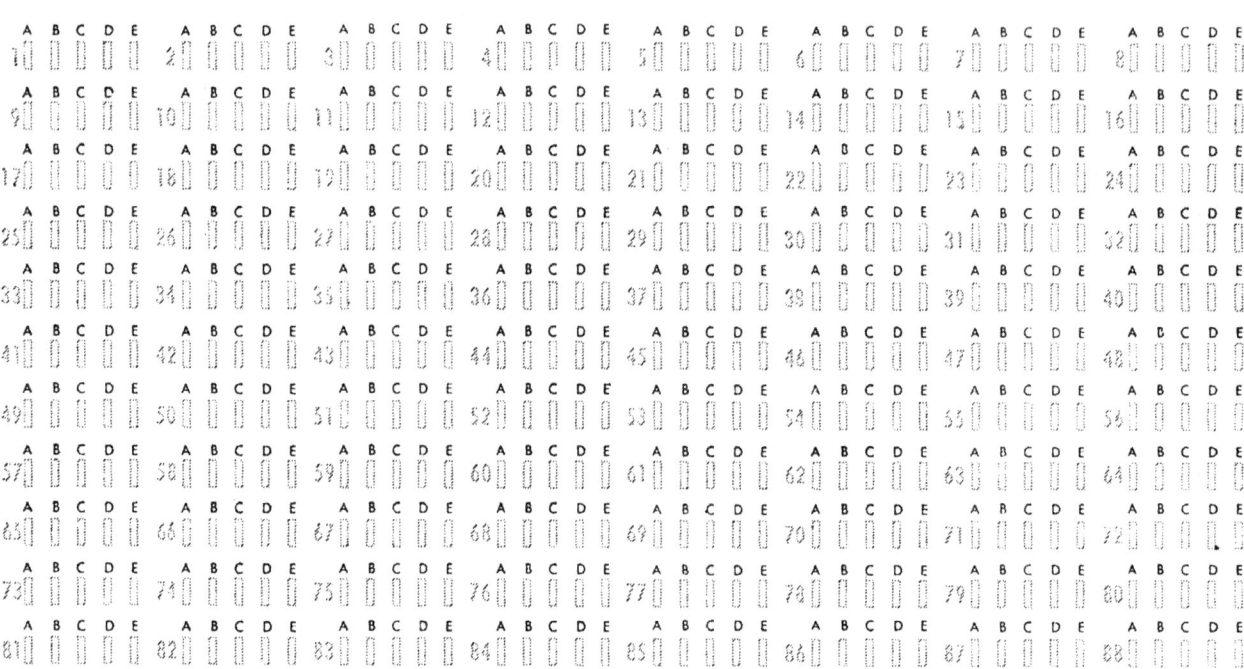

Test-List 2

For each question, mark your answer sheet to show the letter of the box in which the address belongs. Be sure to mark your answers on the answer sheet that you used for Part A. Your answers will go in the section labeled Part B. The first question is numbered 1. You will have 5 *minutes* to do Test—List 2. During the 5 minutes for this list, do not turn to any other page.

1. Cedar
2. 4300–4499 Cliff
3. 4400–4599 Mall
4. Natoma
5. 2300–2999 Laurel
6. 4500–4799 Cliff
7. Ceres
8. 3400–3899 Mall

9. Delhi
10. Dexter
11. 1900–2299 Laurel
12. 3300–3999 Cliff
13. Cicero
14. 4000–4299 Cliff
15. 2100–2799 Mall
16. Foster

17. Magnet
18. Ceres
19. 2800–3399 Mall
20. 3200–3799 Laurel
21. 4300–4499 Cliff
22. Pearl
23. 3900–4399 Mall
24. Natoma

25. 4800–4999 Cliff
26. 1500–1899 Laurel
27. Cedar
28. 4400–4599 Mall
29. 4500–4799 Cliff
30. Dexter
31. 3000–3199 Laurel
32. Niles

33. Delhi
34. 3900–4399 Mall
35. Cicero
36. Dexter
37. 4800–4999 Cliff
38. 2300–2999 Laurel
39. 2100–2799 Mall
40. 3300–3999 Cliff

41. 3400–3899 Mall
42. 4300–4499 Cliff
43. Ceres
44. Foster
45. Magnet
46. 3200–3799 Laurel
47. Pearl
48. 1500–1899 Laurel

49. 4500–4799 Cliff
50. 1900–2299 Laurel
51. Niles
52. 3300–3999 Cliff
53. 2800–3399 Mall
54. Cicero
55. Delhi
56. 4000–4299 Cliff

57. Dexter
58. Magnet
59. 3000–3199 Laurel
60. 3900–4399 Mall
61. Natoma
62. 3000–3199 Laurel
63. 4300–4499 Cliff
64. Cedar

65. 4400–4599 Mall
66. 1500–1899 Laurel
67. 4800–4999 Cliff
68. Delhi
69. Pearl
70. 2300–2999 Laurel
71. 4500–4799 Cliff
72. Niles

73. 4000–4299 Cliff
74. 3400–3899 Mall
75. 1900–2299 Laurel
76. 2800–3399 Mall
77. Ceres
78. Magnet
79. Cicero
80. 3200–3799 Laurel

81. 3000–3199 Laurel
82. 3900–4399 Mall
83. Natoma
84. 3300–3999 Cliff
85. 3400–3899 Mall
86. Foster
87. 2100–2799 Mall
88. 4300–4499 Cliff

STOP.

If you finish before the time is up, go back and rework the questions on this page only.

WHEN THE TIME IS UP, TURN TO THE NEXT PAGE.

Samples for Part C

In this Part there are two kinds of questions. In some questions you will have to say what a word or group of words, that is in italics, means. In other questions you will have to read a paragraph and then answer the questions that follow.

You will have *3 minutes* to study and do the sample questions on this page. Now do the sample questions and mark your answers on the Sample Answer Sheet on this page.

1. The reports were *consolidated* by the secretary. *Consolidated* means most nearly
   - A) combined
   - B) concluded
   - C) distributed
   - D) protected
   - E) weighed

   In this question the word *consolidated* is in italics. So you are to decide which one of the suggested answers means most nearly the same as *consolidated*. "Combined" means most nearly the same as consolidated; so you should have darkened box A for question 1.

2. "Post Office clerks assigned to stamp-windows are directly responsible financially in the selling of postage. In addition, they are expected to have a thorough knowledge as to the acceptability of matter offered for mailing. Any information which they give out to the public must be accurate."

   The paragraph best supports the statement that clerks assigned to stamp-window duty
   - A) must account for stamps issued to them for sale
   - B) have had long training in other post office work
   - C) advise the public only on matters of official business
   - D) must refer continuously to the sources of postal regulations
   - E) inspect the contents of every package offered for mailing

   The statement that is best supported by the paragraph is that "clerks assigned to stamp-window duty must account for stamps issued them for sale." So you should have darkened box A for question 2.

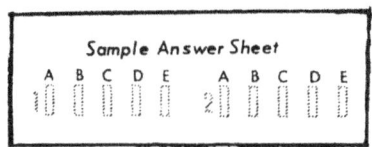

You will have *30 minutes* to do the 32 questions in this part.

DO NOT TURN THIS PAGE UNTIL THE 3 MINUTES FOR IT ARE UP.

PART C

In each of questions 1 through 20, choose the one of the five suggested answers that means most nearly the same as the word or group of words in italics.

Be sure to mark your answers for this part in Part C of the answer sheet.

1. The task *required* his attention. *Required* means most nearly
   A) held
   B) demanded
   C) aroused
   D) increased
   E) revived

2. Employees with previous training *assisted* the others. *Assisted* means most nearly
   A) instructed
   B) warned
   C) stimulated
   D) praised
   E) aided

3. He answered the question *hastily*. *Hastily* means most nearly
   A) incorrectly
   B) nervously
   C) indirectly
   D) bluntly
   E) quickly

4. The signs were *observable* to everyone. *Observable* means most nearly
   A) noticeable
   B) understandable
   C) acceptable
   D) agreeable
   E) available

5. The statements made in the article were *challenged*. *Challenged* means most nearly
   A) misunderstood
   B) disputed
   C) withdrawn
   D) expanded
   E) supported

6. A *trustworthy* messenger was needed to deliver the papers to the inspectors. *Trustworthy* means most nearly
   A) experienced
   B) cautious
   C) industrious
   D) capable
   E) dependable

7. They *endeavored* to keep the rate of production as high as it was when the machines were new. *Endeavor* means most nearly
   A) promised
   B) expected
   C) managed
   D) tried
   E) intended

8. The employee's *accomplishment* was unusually commendable. *Accomplishment* means most nearly
   A) solution
   B) achievement
   C) discovery
   D) proposal
   E) cooperation

9. She is *presumably* the only one who can help you. *Presumably* means most nearly
   A) undoubtedly
   B) practically
   C) probably
   D) reportedly
   E) possibly

10. It would be *advantageous* to begin this job first. *Advantageous* means most nearly
    A) proper
    B) profitable
    C) generous
    D) shrewd
    E) enterprising

11. The organization made a *deliberate* effort to conceal the facts. *Deliberate* means most nearly
    A) intentional
    B) impulsive
    C) desperate
    D) clever
    E) daring

12. The employee was *neglectful of* his responsibilities. *Neglectful of* means most nearly
    A) unworthy of
    B) inattentive to
    C) impatient about
    D) unhappy over
    E) unfit for

13. The foreman gave *specific* orders. *Specific* means most nearly
    A) precise
    B) brief
    C) urgent
    D) fundamental
    E) adequate

14. The procedure to be followed has been *sanctioned*. *Sanctioned* means most nearly
    A) publicly announced
    B) criticized
    C) officially authorized
    D) standardized
    E) carefully planned

15. He contradicted the statement *emphatically*. *Emphatically* means most nearly
    A) eagerly
    B) immediately
    C) positively
    D) reluctantly
    E) repeatedly

16. The trainees were given *minute* directions regarding the work. *Minute* means most nearly
    A) easy
    B) timely
    C) recorded
    D) numerous
    E) detailed

17. The news will bring a prompt *reaction*. *Reaction* means most nearly
    A) response
    B) outburst
    C) admission
    D) recommendation
    E) investigation

18. Only two of the members *participated* in the event. *Participated* means most nearly
    A) advanced
    B) took sides
    C) interfered
    D) took part
    E) argued

19. The facts he presented were *undeniable*. *Undeniable* means most nearly
    A) indefensible
    B) logical
    C) contestable
    D) justifiable
    E) indisputable

20. Attendance at safety lectures is *obligatory*. *Obligatory* means most nearly
    A) optional
    B) important
    C) inconvenient
    D) compulsory
    E) advisable

In each of questions 21 through 32 read the paragraph and then answer the question that follows it.

21. "Iron is used in making our bridges and skyscrapers, subways and steamships, railroads and automobiles, and nearly all kinds of machinery—besides millions of small articles varying from the farmer's scythe to the woman's needle."

    The paragraph best supports the statement that iron
    A) is the most abundant of the metals
    B) has many different uses
    C) is the strongest of all metals
    D) is the only material used in building skyscrapers and bridges
    E) is the most durable of the metals

22. "Some fire-resistant buildings, although wholly constructed of materials that will not burn, may be completely gutted by the spread of fire through their contents by way of hallways and other openings. They may even suffer serious structural damage by the collapse of metal beams and columns."

    The paragraph best supports the statement that some fire-resistant buildings
    A) suffer less damage from fire than from collapse of metal supports
    B) can be damaged seriously by fire
    C) have specially constructed halls and doors
    D) afford less protection to their contents than would ordinary buildings
    E) will burn readily

23. "Life is too short for one person to do very many things well. The person who determines fairly early what he can do that he likes to do, and who goes at it hard and stays with it, is likely to do the best work and find the most peace of mind."

    The paragraph best supports the statement that the reason the average man does not master many different jobs is that he
    A) desires peace of mind
    B) seldom has more than a few interests
    C) is unable to organize his ideas
    D) lacks the necessary time
    E) has a natural tendency to specialize

24. "Both the high school and the college should take the responsibility for preparing the student to get a job. Since the ability to write a good application letter is one of the first steps toward this goal, every teacher should be willing to do what he can to help the student learn to write such letters."

    The paragraph best supports the statement that
    A) inability to write a good letter often reduces one's job prospects
    B) the major responsibility of the school is to obtain jobs for its students
    C) success is largely a matter of the kind of work the student applies for first
    D) every teacher should teach a course in the writing of application letters
    E) letter writing is more important than most subjects taught in high schools and colleges

25. "'White collar' is a term used to describe one of the largest groups of workers in American industry and trade. It distinguishes those who work with the pencil and the mind from those who depend on their hands and the machine. It suggests occupations in which physical exertion and handling of materials are not primary features of the job."

    The paragraph best supports the statement that "white collar" workers are
    A) the most powerful labor group because of their numbers
    B) not so strong physically as those who work with their hands
    C) those who supervise workers handling materials
    D) all whose work is entirely indoors
    E) not likely to use machines so much as are other groups of workers

26. "The location of a railway line is necessarily a compromise between the desire to build the line with as little expense as possible and the desire to construct it so that its route will cover that over which trade and commerce are likely to flow."

    The paragraph best supports the statement that the route selected for a railway line
    A) should be the one over which the line can be built most cheaply
    B) determines the location of commercial centers
    C) should always cover the shortest possible distance between its terminals
    D) cannot always be the one involving the lowest construction costs
    E) is determined chiefly by the kind of production in the area

27. "It is a common assumption that city directories are prepared and published by the cities concerned. However, the directory business is as much a private business as is the publishing of dictionaries and encyclopedias. The companies financing the publication make their profits through the sales of the directories themselves and through the advertising in them."

    The paragraph best supports the statement that
    A) the publication of a city directory is a commercial enterprise
    B) the size of a city directory limits the space devoted to advertising
    C) many city directories are published by dictionary and encyclopedia concerns
    D) city directories are sold at cost to local residents and businessmen
    E) the preparation of a city directory, but not the printing, is a responsibility of the local government

28. "A survey to determine the subjects that have helped students most in their jobs shows that typewriting leads all other subjects in the business group. It also leads among the subjects college students consider most valuable and would take again if they were to return to high school."

    The paragraph best supports the statement that
    A) the ability to type is an asset in business and in school
    B) students who return to night school take typing
    C) students with a knowledge of typing do superior work in college
    D) every person should know how to type
    E) success in business is assured those who can type

29. "Since duplicating machines are being changed constantly, the person who is in the market for such a machine should not purchase offhand the kind with which he is most familiar or the one recommended by the first salesman who calls on him. Instead he should analyze his particular equipment situation and then investigate all the possibilities."

The paragraph best supports the statement that, when duplicating equipment is being purchased,
- A) the purchaser should choose equipment that he can use with the least extra training
- B) the latest models should always be bought
- C) the needs of the purchaser's office should determine the selection
- D) the buyer should have his needs analyzed by an office-equipment salesman
- E) the recommendations of salesmen should usually be ignored

30. "There has been a slump in first-aid training in the industries, and yet one should not fall into the error of thinking there is less interest in first aid in industry. The falling off has been in the number of new employees needing such training. It appears that in industries interested in first-aid training there is now actually a higher percentage so trained than there ever was before."

The paragraph best supports the statement that first-aid training is
- A) a means of avoiding the more serious effects of accidents
- B) being abandoned because of expense
- C) helpful in every line of work
- D) of great importance to employees
- E) sometimes given new workers in industry

31. "There exists a false but popular idea that a clue is a mysterious fact which most people overlook but which some very keen investigator easily discovers and recognizes as having, in itself, a remarkable meaning. The clue is most often an ordinary fact which an observant person picks up—something which gains its significance when, after a long series of careful investigations, it is connected with a network of other clues."

The paragraph best supports the statement that to be of value clues must be
- A) discovered by skilled investigators
- B) found under mysterious circumstances
- C) connected with other facts
- D) discovered soon after the crime
- E) observed many times

32. "It is wise to choose a duplicating machine that will do the work required with the greatest efficiency and at the least cost. Users with a large volume of business need speedy machines that cost little to operate and are well made."

The paragraph best supports the statement that
- A) most users of duplicating machines prefer low operating cost to efficiency
- B) a well-built machine will outlast a cheap one
- C) a duplicating machine is not efficient unless it is sturdy
- D) a duplicating machine should be both efficient and economical
- E) in duplicating machines speed is more usual than low operating cost

STOP.

If you finish before the time is up, check your answers to Part C. Do not go to any other part.

WHEN THE TIME IS UP, TURN TO PAGE 17.

Samples for Part D

In each of the questions in this Part, there is at the left a series of numbers which follow some definite order and, at the right, five sets of two numbers each.

You are to look at the numbers in the series at the left and find out what order they follow. Then decide what the next two numbers in that series would be if the same order were continued. Next find these two numbers in one of the sets at the right, and darken the box on your answer sheet which has the same letter as the answer you select.

Samples

Now do sample question 1. Mark your answer in the space for question 1 on the Sample Answer Sheet on this page.

1. 1 2 3 4 5 6 7... A) 1 2 B) 5 6 C) 8 9 D) 4 5 E) 7 8

The numbers in this series are increasing by 1. If the series were continued for two more numbers, it would read: 1 2 3 4 5 6 7 8 9. Therefore the correct answer is 8 and 9, and you should have darkened C on the Sample Answer Sheet for question 1.

2. 15 14 13 12 11 10 9. . A) 2 1 B) 17 16 C) 8 9 D) 8 7 E) 9 8

The numbers in this series are decreasing by 1. If the series were continued for two more numbers, it would read: 15 14 13 12 11 10 9 8 7. Therefore the correct answer is 8 and 7, and you should have darkened D on the Sample Answer Sheet for question 2.

3. 20 20 21 21 22 22 23....... A) 23 23 B) 23 24 C) 19 19 D) 22 23 E) 21 22

Each number in this series is repeated and then increased by 1. If the series were continued for two more numbers, it would read: 20 20 21 21 22 22 23 23 24. Therefore the correct answer is 23 and 24, and you should have darkened B on the Sample Answer Sheet for question 3.

4. 17 3 17 4 17 5 17.......... A) 6 17 B) 6 7 C) 17 6 D) 5 6 E) 17 7

This series is the number 17 separated by numbers increasing by 1, beginning with the number 3. If the series were continued for two more numbers, it would read: 17 3 17 4 17 5 17 6 17. Therefore the correct answer is 6 and 17, and you should have darkened A on the Sample Answer Sheet for question 4.

5. 1 2 4 5 7 8 10............. A) 11 12 B) 12 14 C) 10 13 D) 12 13 E) 11 13

The numbers in this series are increasing first by 1 (that is plus 1) and then by 2 (that is plus 2). If the series were continued for two more numbers, it would read: 1 2 4 5 7 8 10 (plus 1) which is *11* (plus 2) which is *13*. Therefore the correct answer is 11 and 13, and you should have darkened E on the Sample Answer Sheet for question 5.

Now you will have *10 minutes* to read and work sample questions 6 through 18. Mark your answers on the Sample Answer Sheets.

6. 21 21 20 20 19 19 18....... A) 18 18 B) 18 17 C) 17 18 D) 17 17 E) 18 19

7. 1 22 1 23 1 24 1........... A) 26 1 B) 25 26 C) 25 1 D) 1 26 E) 1 25

8. 1 20 3 19 5 18 7........... A) 8 9 B) 8 17 C) 17 10 D) 17 9 E) 9 18

9. 4 7 10 13 16 19 22......... A) 23 26 B) 25 27 C) 25 26 D) 25 28 E) 24 27

10. 30 2 28 4 26 6 24.......... A) 23 9 B) 26 8 C) 8 9 D) 26 22 E) 8 22

Explanations for questions 6 through 10.

6. Each number in the series repeats itself and then decreases by 1 or minus 1; *21* (repeat) *21* (minus 1) which makes *20* (repeat) *20* (minus 1) which makes *19* (repeat) *19* (minus 1) which makes *18* (repeat) ? (minus 1) ?
7. The number 1 is separated by numbers which begin with 22 and increase by 1; *1 22 1* (increase 22 by 1) which makes *23 1* (increase 23 by 1) which makes *24 1* (increase 24 by 1) which makes ?
8. This is best explained by two alternating series—one series starts with *1* and increases by 2 or plus 2; the other series starts with *20* and decreases by 1 or minus 1.

$$1 \uparrow 3 \uparrow 5 \uparrow 7 \uparrow ?$$
$$20 \quad 19 \quad 18 \quad ?$$

9. This series of numbers increases by 3 (plus 3) beginning with the first number. *4* (plus 3) *7* (plus 3) *10* (plus 3) *13* (plus 3) *16* (plus 3) *19* (plus 3) *22* (plus 3) ? (plus 3) ?
10. Look for two alternating series—one series starts with 30 and decreases by 2 (minus 2), the other series starts with 2 and increases by 2 (plus 2).

$$30 \uparrow 28 \uparrow 26 \uparrow 24 \uparrow ?$$
$$2 \quad 4 \quad 6 \quad ?$$

The correct answers to sample questions 6 through 10 are: 6B, 7C, 8D, 9D, and 10E.

Now try questions 11 to 18.

11. 5 6 20 7 8 19 9 . . . . A) 10 18 B) 18 17 C) 10 17 D) 18 19 E) 10 11
12. 9 10 1 11 12 2 13 . . . . A) 2 4   B) 3 14   C) 14 3   D) 14 15   E) 14 1
13. 4 6 9 11 14 16 19 . . . . A) 21 24 B) 22 25 C) 20 22 D) 21 23 E) 22 24
14. 8 8 1 10 10 3 12 . . . . A) 13 13 B) 12 5   C) 12 4   D) 13 5   E) 4 12
15. 14 1 2 15 3 4 16 . . . . A) 5 16   B) 6 7   C) 5 17   D) 5 6   E) 17 5
16. 10 12 50 15 17 50 20 . . . . A) 50 21 B) 21 50 C) 50 22 D) 22 50 E) 22 24
17. 1 2 3 50 4 5 6 51 7 8 . . . . A) 9 10   B) 9 52   C) 51 10 D) 10 52 E) 10 50
18. 20 21 23 24 27 28 32 33 38 39 . . . . . A) 45 46 B) 45 52 C) 44 45 D) 44 49 E) 40 46

Hints for questions 11 through 18.

11. Alternating series: *5 6* ↑ *7 8* ↑ *9* ? ↑
                            20   19   ?
12. Alternating series: *9 10* ↑ *11 12* ↑ *13* ? ↑
                            1   2   ?
13. Increases alternately by 2 (plus 2) then 3 (plus 3)—*4* (plus 2) *6* (plus 3) *9* (plus 2) *11* (plus 3) *14* (plus 2) *16* (plus 3) *19* (plus 2) ? (plus 3) ?
14. Alternating series: *8 8* ↑ *10 10* ↑ *12* ? ↑
                            1   3   ?
15. Alternating series: *14* ↑ ↑ *15* ↑ ↑ *16* ↑ ↑
                           1 2   3 4   ? ?
16. Alternating series: *10 12* ↑ *15 17* ↑ *20* ? ↑
                           50   50   ?
17. Alternating series: *1 2 3* ↑ *4 5 6* ↑ *7 8* ? ↑
                           50   51   ?
18. Increases alternately by (plus 1), (plus 2), (plus 1), (plus 3), (plus 1), (plus 4), etc.—*20* (plus 1) *21* (plus 2) *23* (plus 1) *24* (plus 3) *27* (plus 1) *28* (plus 4) *32* (plus 1) *33* (plus 5) *38* (plus 1) *39* (plus 6) ? (plus 1) ?

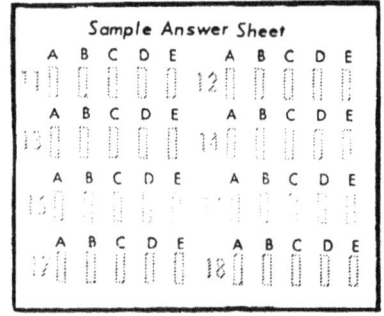

Sample Answer Sheet

The correct answers to the sample questions above are: 11A, 12C, 13A, 14B, 15D, 16D, 17B, and 18A.

On the test you will have *30 minutes* to answer as many of the 24 questions as you can.

DO NOT TURN THIS PAGE UNTIL THE TIME FOR THE SAMPLE QUESTIONS IS UP.

PART D

In each series below determine what the order of the numbers at the left is, and decide what the next two numbers should be. From the suggested answers at the right, choose the one that gives the next two numbers in the series and darken the box on the answer sheet with the same letter as your answer. (If the two numbers you have decided upon are not there, do the problem again.) Answer first the questions that are easiest for you; then answer the other ones.

Be sure to mark your answers in Part D of your answer sheet.

		A)	B)	C)	D)	E)
1.	8 9 10 8 9 10 8............	8 9	9 10	9 8	10 8	8 10
2.	3 4 4 3 5 5 3...............	3 3	6 3	3 6	6 6	6 7
3.	7 7 3 7 7 4 7...............	7 7	7 8	5 7	8 7	7 5
4.	18 18 19 20 20 21 22.......	22 23	23 24	23 23	22 22	21 22
5.	2 6 10 3 7 11 4............	12 16	5 9	8 5	12 5	8 12
6.	11 8 15 12 19 16 23........	27 20	24 20	27 24	20 24	20 27
7.	16 8 15 9 14 10 13.........	12 11	13 12	11 13	11 12	11 14
8.	4 5 13 6 7 12 8.............	9 11	13 9	9 13	11 9	11 10
9.	3 8 4 9 5 10 6 11 7........	7 11	7 8	11 8	12 7	12 8
10.	18 14 19 17 20 20 21......	22 24	14 19	24 21	21 23	23 22
11.	6 9 10 7 11 12 8............	9 10	9 13	16 14	13 14	14 15
12.	7 5 3 9 7 5 11..............	13 12	7 5	9 7	13 7	9 9
13.	7 9 18 10 12 18 13.........	18 14	15 18	14 15	15 14	14 18
14.	2 6 4 8 6 10 8..............	12 10	6 10	10 12	12 16	6 4
15.	7 9 12 14 17 19 22.........	25 27	23 24	23 25	24 27	26 27
16.	3 23 5 25 7 27 9...........	10 11	27 29	29 11	11 28	28 10
17.	18 17 16 14 13 12 10.......	9 8	6 7	8 6	8 7	10 9
18.	5 7 8 10 11 13 14 16.......	18 19	17 18	18 20	17 19	19 20
19.	28 27 25 24 22 21 19.......	18 16	17 16	18 17	17 15	20 18
20.	2 2 4 6 6 8 10.............	12 12	12 14	10 10	10 8	10 12
21.	2 7 3 8 4 9 5...............	6 7	10 6	6 10	10 11	5 10
22.	19 18 16 21 20 18 23.......	20 25	25 20	22 25	22 20	25 22
23.	3 5 7 7 4 6 8 8 5 7 9......	9 6	6 6	6 9	10 8	8 10
24.	15 26 24 16 21 19 17 16 14 18..	17 15	11 9	15 14	17 16	11 10

If you finish before the time is up, check your answers to Part D. Do not go to any other part.

CORRECT ANSWERS FOR CLERK-CARRIER TEST

EXAMINATION SECTION
TEST 1

Memory for Addresses Test

DIRECTIONS: In this test you will have to memorize the locations (A, B, C, D or E) of 25 addresses shown in five boxes. For example, "Sardis" is in box "C," "4300-4799 West" is in box "E," etc. Study the locations of the addresses for five minutes (try sounding them to yourself), then cover the boxes and try to answer the questions below. *PRINT THE LETTER OF THE CORRECT ANSWER IN THE SPACE AT THE RIGHT.*

Box A	Box B	Box C
4700-5599 Table	6800-6999 Table	5600-6499 Table
Lismore	Kelford	Joel
4800-5199 West	5200-5799 West	3200-3499 West
Hesper	Musella	Sardis
5500-6399 Blake	4800-5499 Blake	6400-7299 Blake

Box D	Box E
6500-6799 Table	4400-4699 Table
Tatum	Ruskin
3500-4299 West	4300-4799 West
Porter	Somers
4300-4799 Blake	7300-7499 Blake

1. Musella   1._____
2. 4300-4799 Blake   2._____
3. 4700-5599 Table   3._____
4. Tatum   4._____
5. 5500-6399 Blake   5._____
6. Hesper   6._____
7. Kelford   7._____
8. Somers   8._____
9. 6400-7299 Blake   9._____
10. Joel   10._____
11. 5500-6399 Blake   11._____
12. 5200-5799 West   12._____
13. Porter   13._____
14. 7300-7499 Blake   14._____

KEY (CORRECT ANSWERS)

1. B
2. D
3. A
4. D
5. A
6. A
7. B
8. E
9. C
10. C
11. A
12. B
13. D
14. E

TEST 2

Address Checking Test

DIRECTIONS: In this test you will have to decide whether two addresses are alike or different. If the two addresses are exactly alike in every way, mark the answer "A." If the two addresses are different, mark the answer "D." *PRINT THE LETTER OF THE CORRECT ANSWER IN THE SPACE AT THE RIGHT.*

1.	2134 S. 20th St.	2134 S. 20th St.	1._____
2.	4608 N. Warnock St.	4806 N. Warnock St.	2._____
3.	1202 W. Girard Dr.	1202 W. Girard Rd.	3._____
4.	Chappaqua, NY 10514	Chappaqua, NY 10514	4._____
5.	2207 Markland Ave.	2207 Markham Ave.	5._____

General Test

DIRECTIONS: In this test there are three kinds of questions—Vocabulary, Reading and Number Series. For Vocabulary questions, like number 6, choose the suggested answer that means most nearly the same as the word or words in italics. For Reading questions, like number 7, read the paragraph and answer the question that follows it. For Number Series questions, like numbers 8 through 25, there is a series of numbers which is arranged in some definite order or pattern, followed by five sets of two numbers each. Determine the order or pattern of the numbers at the left and choose from the selections below the two numbers that would properly continue the order or pattern. *PRINT THE LETTER OF THE CORRECT ANSWER IN THE SPACE AT THE RIGHT.*

6. The reports were *consolidated by* the secretary. *Consolidated* most nearly means   6._____

    A. combined   B. concluded   C. distributed   D. protected   E. weighed

7. "Post office clerks assigned to stamp windows are directly responsible financially in the selling of postage. In addition, they are expected to have a thorough knowledge as to the acceptability of matter offered for mailing. Any information which they give out to the public must be accurate."   7._____
The paragraph best supports the statement that clerks assigned to stamp-window duty

    A. must account for stamps issued to them for sale
    B. have had long training in other post-office work
    C. advise the public only on matters of official business
    D. must refer continuously to the sources of postal regulations
    E. inspect the contents of every package offered for mailing

8. 1 2 3 4 5 6 7 ...   8._____

    A. 1 2   B. 5 6   C. 8 9
    D. 4 5   E. 7 8

9. 15 14 13 12 11 10 9 ...

    A. 2 1
    B. 17 16
    C. 8 9
    D. 8 7
    E. 9 8

10. 20 20 21 21 22 22 23 ...

    A. 23 23
    B. 23 24
    C. 19 19
    D. 22 23
    E. 21 22

11. 17 3 17 4 17 5 17 ...

    A. 6 17
    B. 6 7
    C. 17 6
    D. 5 6
    E. 17 7

12. 1 2 4 5 7 8 10 ...

    A. 11 12
    B. 12 14
    C. 10 13
    D. 12 13
    E. 11 13

13. 21 21 20 20 19 19 18 ...

    A. 18 18
    B. 18 17
    C. 17 18
    D. 17 17
    E. 18 19

14. 1 22 1 23 1 24 1 ...

    A. 26 1
    B. 25 26
    C. 25 1
    D. 1 26
    E. 1 25

15. 1 20 3 19 5 18 7 ...

    A. 8 9
    B. 8 17
    C. 17 10
    D. 17 9
    E. 9 18

16. 4 7 10 13 16 19 22 ...

    A. 23 26
    B. 25 27
    C. 25 26
    D. 25 28
    E. 24 27

17. 30 2 28 4 26 6 24 ...

    A. 23 9
    B. 26 8
    C. 8 9
    D. 26 22
    E. 8 22

18. 5 6 20 7 8 19 9 ...

    A. 10 18
    B. 18 17
    C. 10 7
    D. 18 19
    E. 10 11

19. 9 10 1 11 12 2 13 ...

    A. 2 14
    B. 3 14
    C. 14 3
    D. 14 15
    E. 14 1

20. 4 6 9 11 14 16 19 ...

    A. 21 24
    B. 22 25
    C. 20 22
    D. 21 23
    E. 22 24

21. 8 8 1 10 10 3 12 ...   21._____
    A. 13 13   B. 12 5   C. 12 4
    D. 13 5   E. 4 12

22. 14 1 2 15 3 4 16...   22._____
    A. 5 16   B. 6 7   C. 5 17
    D. 5 6   E. 17 5

23. 10 12 50 15 17 50 20 ...   23._____
    A. 50 21   B. 21 50   C. 50 22
    D. 22 50   E. 22 24

24. 1 2 3 50 4 5 6 51 7 8...   24._____
    A. 9 10   B. 9 52   C. 51 10
    D. 10 52   E. 10 50

25. 20 21 23 24 27 28 32 33 38 39 ...   25._____
    A. 45 46   B. 45 52   C. 44 45
    D. 44 49   E. 40 46

KEY (CORRECT ANSWERS)

1. A   11. A
2. D   12. E
3. D   13. B
4. A   14. C
5. D   15. D

6. A   16. D
7. A   17. E
8. C   18. A
9. D   19. C
10. B   20. A

21. B
22. D
23. D
24. B
25. A

SAMPLE MAIL HANDLER TEST

Now that you have studied the instructions and taken the practice tests in this book, you are ready to take the Sample Tests. There is one Sample Test for Mail Handler.

The Sample Tests are exactly like the ones you will have to take in the examinations. The time allowances and the numbers of questions are the same as they are in the real tests.

At the back of the book you will find some answer sheets to use. These answer sheets are like the ones you will use in the examinations.

It is a good idea to have a friend tell you when the time is up for each set of sample questions and each part of the test. (There are sample questions for each part.) When you take the Sample Mail Handler Test, you should have a friend read the material in the Following Oral Directions Booklet, which is pages 13 - 15.

After you have finished answering the questions for a sample test, compare your answers with the correct answers for that test and see how well you did.

Mail Handler Test

Time Required for Each Part

    Part A

        Samples   3 minutes

        Test   6 minutes

    Part B

        Samples and Test   Approximately 25 minutes

    Part C

        Samples   3 minutes

        Test   25 minutes

INTERPRETATION OF TEST SCORES ON SAMPLE MAIL HANDLER TEST

After you have taken a Part of the test, or after you have finished the test, compare your answers with those given in the Correct Answers to Sample Test. You will find them on page 12.

For the Address Checking (Part A), count the number that you got right and the number that you got wrong. (If you didn't mark anything for a question, it doesn't get counted.)

    From the number right
    Subtract the number wrong
    This number (the difference) is your score———————→

The meaning of the score is as follows:

    52 or higher... Good.
    Between 32 and 51................................... Fair.
    Below 32.. You need more practice.

Go back and see where you made your mistakes. Were you careless? Did you work too slowly?

For the Following Oral Directions (Part B), your score is the number right: _____.

The meaning of the score is as follows:

    28 or higher... Good.
    Between 24 and 27................................... Fair.
    Below 24.. You need more practice.

For the Word Meaning (Part C), your score is the number right: _____.

The meaning of the score is as follows:

    24 or higher... Good.
    Between 20 and 23................................... Fair.
    Below 20.. You need more practice.

Go back and see where you made your mistakes. Were you careless? Were there words that you didn't know? If you didn't know the words, try to build up your vocabulary. Some ways of doing this are suggested previously.

SAMPLE MAIL HANDLER TEST

There are three parts to this test. It is best for a friend to time this test for you. (The correct time limits for each part are listed on page 1.) Be sure not to take any more or any less time than given in the instructions for each part.

Tear out an answer sheet from the back of this book and use it to mark your answers for each part.

Directions and Samples for Part A

In this Part you will be given addresses to compare. You are to mark your answer for each question in the row, on your separate answer sheet, that has the same number as the number of the question.

If the two addresses are exactly *Alike* in every way, darken box A. If the two addresses are *Different* in any way, darken box D.

Here are some sample questions for you to do. Mark your answers to them on the Sample Answer Sheet on this page. You should not take more than *3 minutes* to read and study the material on this page of the test.

Keep your mark inside the box on the answer sheet. If you want to change an answer, erase the mark you don't want to count. Then mark your new answer. It will be to your advantage to work as quickly and accurately as possible since your score on this Part will be based on the number of wrong answers as well as the number of right answers. It is not expected that you will be able to finish all the questions in the time allowed.

Be sure to use a No. 2 (medium) pencil.

1 ... Acme La   Acme La

Since the two addresses are exactly alike, you should have darkened box A for question 1 on the Sample Answer Sheet. Now do the other sample questions.

2 ... Orleans Mass   Orleans Mich
3 ... Saxe Va   Saxis Va
4 ... Chappaqua N Y 10514   Chappaqua N Y 10514
5 ... Los Angeles Calif 90013   Los Angeles Calif 90018

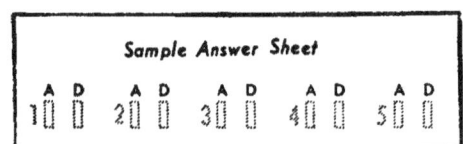

Now compare your answers with the Correct Answers to Sample Questions. If your answers are not the same as the correct answers shown, go back and study the samples to see where you made a mistake.

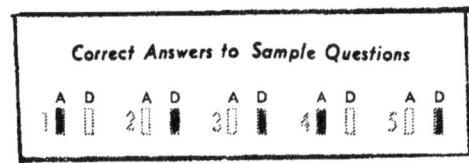

When you begin the test, work as fast as you can without making mistakes. Do as many questions as you can in the time allowed.

Look at your answer sheet. The answers to this part of the examination must be marked in **Part A** of the answer sheet. Notice also that the answer spaces are numbered across the page. Mark the answer for question 1 in space 1.

You will have *6 minutes* to answer as many of the 95 questions as you can.

DO NOT TURN THIS PAGE UNTIL YOU ARE READY TO BEGIN THE TEST.

PART A

REMEMBER: Mark your answers on the separate answer sheet. Use "A" for "Alike" and "D" for "Different." Work as quickly as you can.

1 ...	Las Vegas Nev	Las Vegas N Mex
2 ...	New Sarpy La	New Sarpy La
3 ...	Loma Mont	Loma Mont
4 ...	Pitsburg Ohio	Pitsburg Ohio
5 ...	Bloomington Ind	Bloomingdale Ind
6 ...	Eastabuchie Miss	Eastabuchie Minn
7 ...	Newberg Oreg	Newberg Oreg
8 ...	Arco Ga	Atco Ga
9 ...	Orocovis P R	Orocovis P R
10 ...	Bloomingburg Ohio	Bloomingdale Ohio
11 ...	Crumpton Md	Crampton Md
12 ...	Nashville Tenn 37214	Nashville Tenn 37214
13 ...	Charlson N Dak	Charlson N Dak
14 ...	Florence S C	Florence S Dak
15 ...	Burnett Minn	Barnett Minn
16 ...	Lakewood Wash	Lakewood Wash
17 ...	Moodus Conn	Moosup Conn
18 ...	Brighton N Y 11200	Brighton N Y 14600
19 ...	Akiak Alaska	Aniak Alaska
20 ...	Maskell Nebr	Maskell Nebr
21 ...	Gaston S C	Gasden S C
22 ...	Sonora Calif 95370	Sonora Calif 95310
23 ...	Glovergap W Va	Clovergap W Va
24 ...	Fairfax Ala	Fairfield Ala
25 ...	Cubero N Mex	Cubero N Mex
26 ...	Reedsville Wis	Reeseville Wis
27 ...	Ada Ohio	Ava Ohio
28 ...	Cheektowaga N Y 14278	Cheektowaga N Y 14278
29 ...	Cayuga N Y	Cayuta N Y
30 ...	Fruitland Idaho	Fruitland Idaho
31 ...	Cora W Va	Cord W Va
32 ...	Afton Tex	Anton Tex
33 ...	Hamptonville N C	Hamptonville N C
34 ...	Portola Calif 96100	Portola Calif 96100
35 ...	Sonoita Ariz	Sonoita Ariz
36 ...	Dunbarton N H 03300	Dunbarton N H 03300
37 ...	Benson Ill	Benton Ill
38 ...	Portland Oreg 97206	Portland Oreg 97206
39 ...	Flayton N Dak	Flaston N Dak
40 ...	Barnsdall Okla	Barnsdall Okla
41 ...	Irmo S C	Irmo S C
42 ...	East Barnet Vt	East Barnet Vt
43 ...	Ellenburg Center N Y 12900	Ellenburg Depot N Y 12900
44 ...	Helena Mo	Helena Mo
45 ...	Grafton Wis	Granton Wis
46 ...	Columbia N C	Columbus N C
47 ...	Dumont Colo	Dupont Colo

GO ON TO NUMBER 48 ON THE NEXT PAGE.

48 ...	McClusky N Dak	McClosky N Dak
49 ...	Sheldon S C	Shelton S C
50 ...	Fredericksburg Iowa	Fredericksburg Iowa
51 ...	Holden Vt	Holton Vt
52 ...	Karlsruhe N Dak	Karlsruhe N Dak
53 ...	East Springfield Pa	West Springfield Pa
54 ...	Villa Prades P R	Villa Prades P R
55 ...	Cadmus Mich	Cadmus Mich
56 ...	New London N H 03200	New London N H 03200
57 ...	Anchorage Alaska 95501	Anchorage Alaska 99501
58 ...	Garciasville Tex 78547	Garciasville Tex 78547
59 ...	Edenton Ohio	Edenton Ohio
60 ...	Vernal Utah	Vernon Utah
61 ...	Tullahassee Okla	Tallahassee Okla
62 ...	Carlton Wash	Carson Wash
63 ...	Tucson Ariz 85721	Tucson Ariz 85751
64 ...	Vermillion S Dak 57069	Vermillion S Dak 57069
65 ...	Oxford N H	Orford N H
66 ...	Evanston Wyo	Evanston Wyo
67 ...	Gonzalez Fla 32560	Gonzalez Fla 32560
68 ...	Clifton Tenn	Clinton Tenn
69 ...	Lindsborg Kans	Lindsborg Kans
70 ...	Greenbush Va	Greenbush Va
71 ...	Paterson N J 07400	Paterson N J 07500
72 ...	Monticello Minn	Monticello Minn
73 ...	Haina Hawaii	Hana Hawaii
74 ...	Barre Mass	Barre Mass
75 ...	Beech Creek Ky 42300	Beech Grove Ky 42300
76 ...	Biddeford Maine 04005	Biddeford Maine 04006
77 ...	Richford N Y	Richland N Y
78 ...	Shamko Oreg 97057	Shaneko Oreg 97057
79 ...	Farmington N Mex	Framington N Mex
80 ...	Goodwell Okla	Goodwell Okla
81 ...	Saginaw Tex	Saginaw Tex
82 ...	Jersey City N J 07323	Jersey City N J 07328
83 ...	Fremont N C	Fremont N C
84 ...	Ottumwa S Dak	Ottumwa S Dak
85 ...	Alasha S Dak	Alaska S Dak
86 ...	Oklahoma City Okla 73106	Oklahoma City Okla 73106
87 ...	Slocum R I	Slocam R I
88 ...	Leesburg Va	Leesburg Va
89 ...	Wilmot Ark	Wilmor Ark
90 ...	Seaford Del 19973	Seaford Del 19973
91 ...	Aldan Pa	Alden Pa
92 ...	Washington D C 20008	Washington D C 20018
93 ...	Wilson Ark	Wilton Ark
94 ...	Fresno Calif 93705	Fresno Calif 93705
95 ...	Clearmont Wyo	Clearmont Wyo

STOP.

If you finish before the time is up, check your answers to this part. Do not go to any other part.

PART B

Part B of the Mail Handler Test is a test of following oral directions. In this Part, have a friend read the directions to you. The instructions, or directions, to be read to you are on pages 13-15. This part of the test will take approximately 25 minutes.

Below are some sample questions as well as a Sample Answer Sheet. Your friend will read the directions to you. Listen carefully.

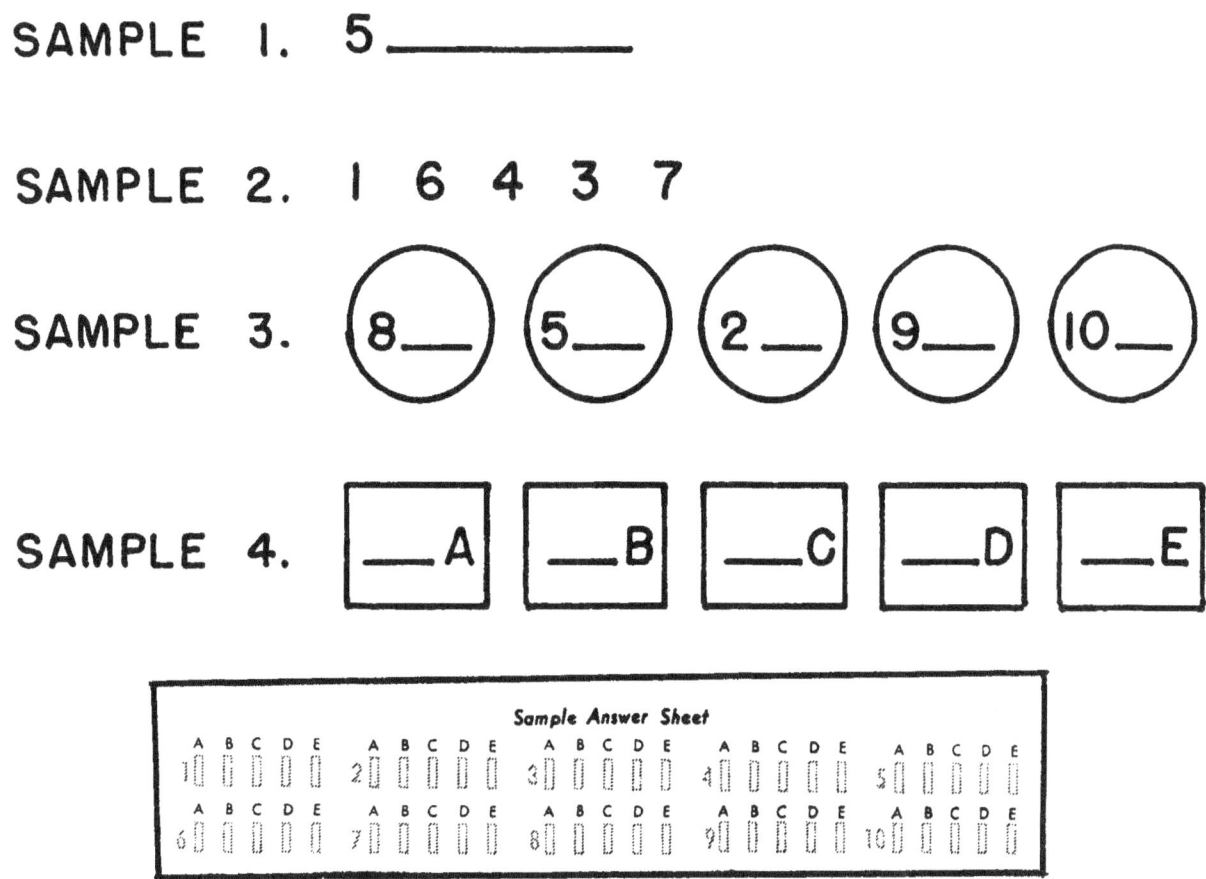

DO NOT GO ON TO THE NEXT PAGE UNTIL YOU ARE TOLD TO DO SO.

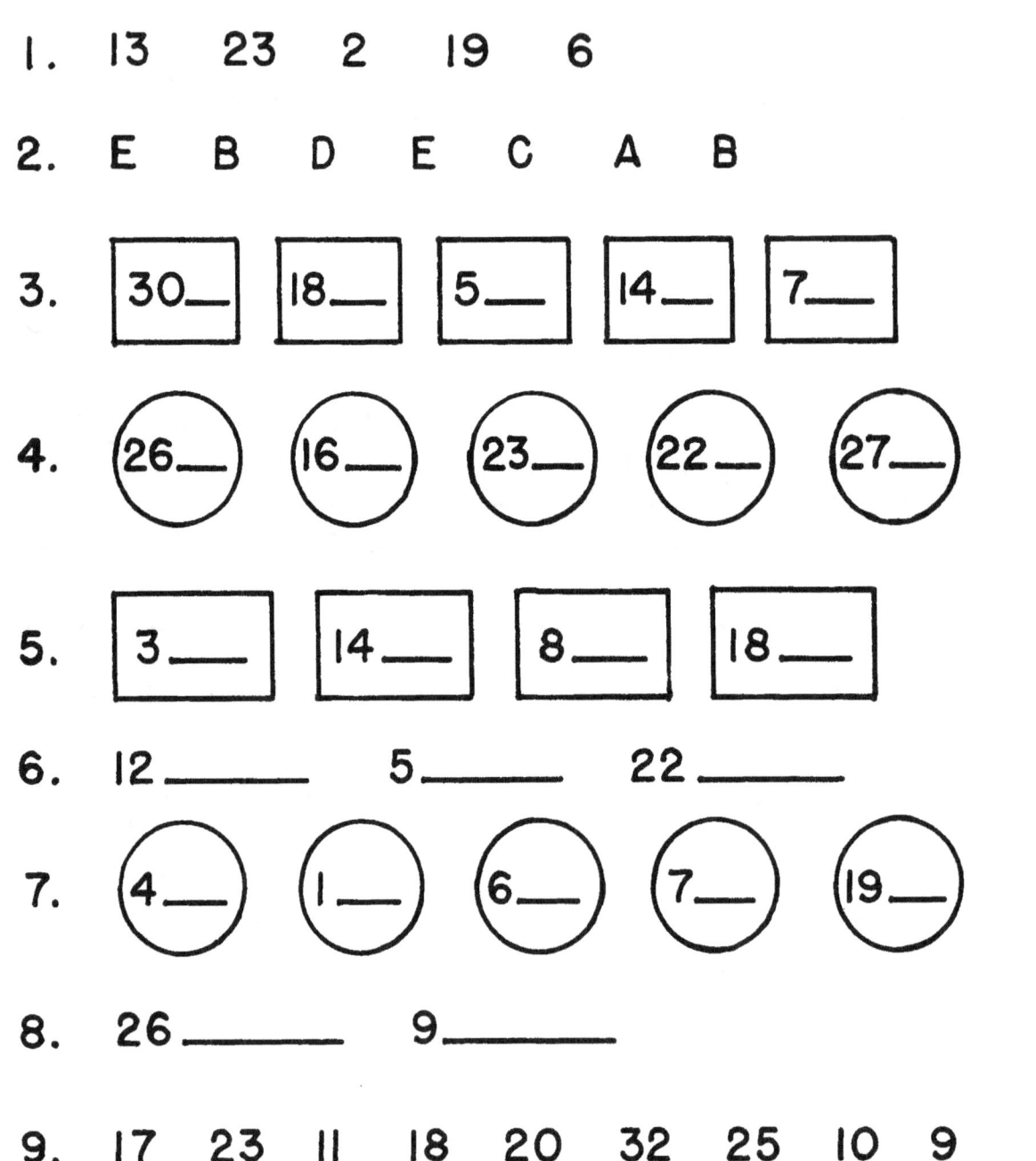

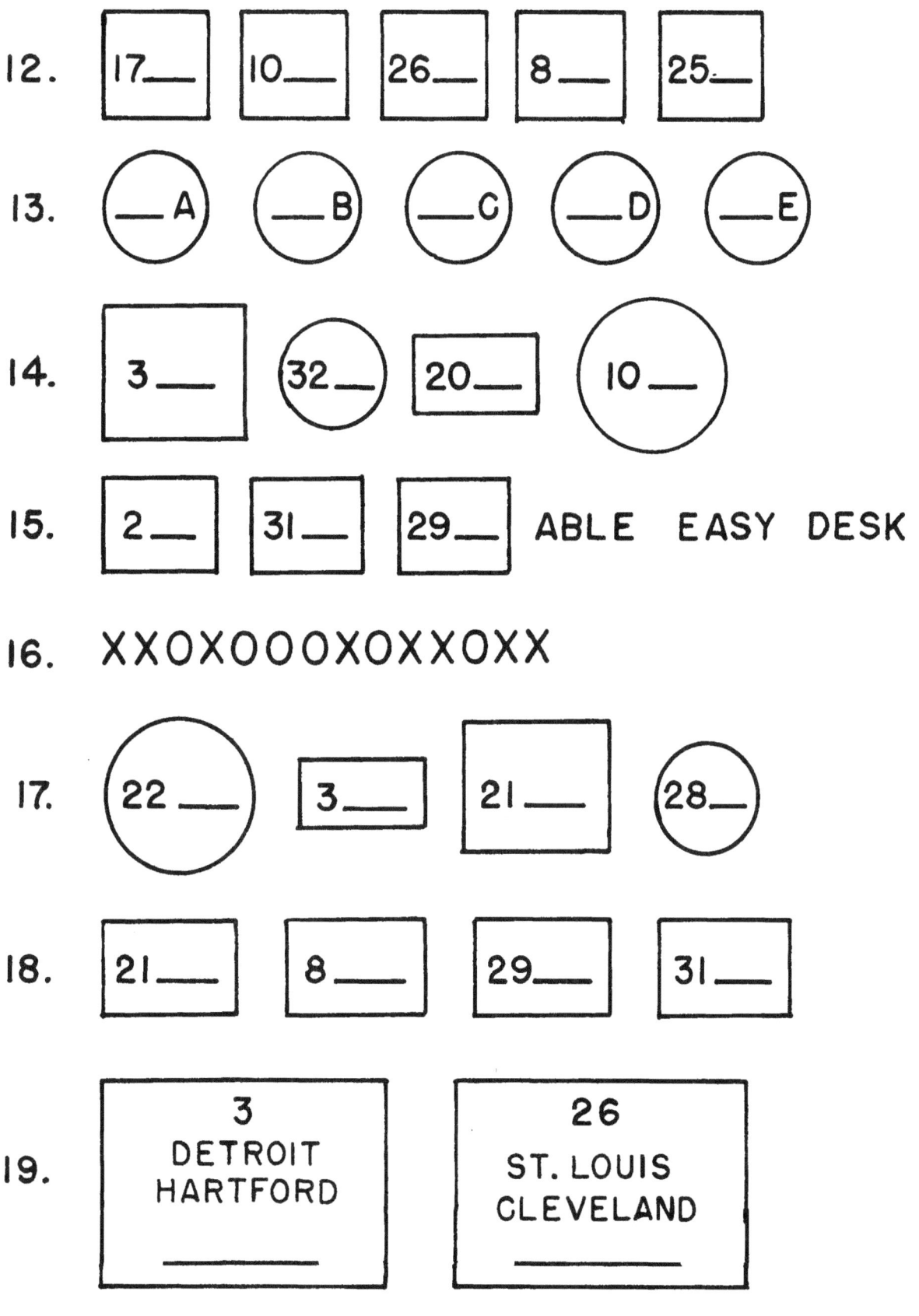

Sample Questions for Part C

In each question in Part C you are asked what a word or phrase means. In each question a word or phrase is in italics. Five other words or phrases—lettered A, B, C, D, and E—are given as possible meanings of the word or phrase in italics. Only one is *right*. You are to pick out the one that is right. Then on the answer sheet, find the answer space numbered the same as the question, and darken the box under the letter of the right answer.

Here are some sample questions for you to do. Mark your answers to them on the Sample Answer Sheet on this page. Do not spend more than *3 minutes* on reading and studying this page.

1. The letter was *short*. *Short* means most nearly
    A) tall
    B) wide
    C) brief
    D) heavy
    E) dark

   In this question the word *short* is in italics. So you are to decide which one of the suggested answers means most nearly the same as *short*. "Brief" means most nearly the same as *short*; so you should have darkened box C for question 1.

2. A crane was used to *raise* the heavy part. *Raise* means most nearly
    A) lift
    B) drag
    C) drop
    D) deliver
    E) guide

   Darken the box for your answer. Then compare the answers you have marked with those given in the Correct Answers to Sample Questions.

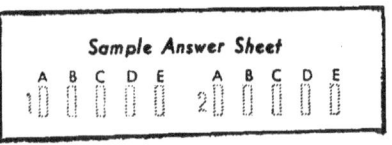

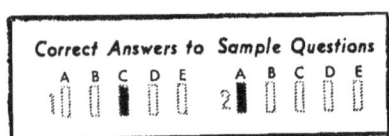

Try to answer every question in this part. Answer first the questions that are easiest for you. Then do the others. If you are not sure of an answer, guess.

You will have *25 minutes* to answer the 32 questions in this part. If you finish before the time is up, go back and check your answers for Part C.

You are to mark your answers to these questions in Part C of your answer sheet.

DO NOT TURN THIS PAGE UNTIL YOU ARE READY TO BEGIN PART C.

PART C

In each question in this part, choose the one of the five suggested answers that means most nearly the same as the word in italics.

Be sure to mark your answers for this part in Part C of the answer sheet.

1. He was asked to *speak* at the meeting. *Speak* means most nearly
   A) vote
   B) explain
   C) talk
   D) shout
   E) decide

2. They *discovered* the missing boxes in the morning. *Discovered* means most nearly
   A) sought
   B) found
   C) opened
   D) noticed
   E) inspected

3. The number of letters mailed by this office is *double* what it was last year. *Double* means most nearly
   A) twice
   B) different from
   C) more than
   D) almost
   E) the same as

4. The post office had to *purchase* the new equipment. *Purchase* means most nearly
   A) charge
   B) construct
   C) supply
   D) buy
   E) order

5. The shell was *hollow*. *Hollow* means most nearly
   A) smooth
   B) hard
   C) soft
   D) rough
   E) empty

6. The packages were kept in a *secure* place. *Secure* means most nearly
   A) distant
   B) safe
   C) convenient
   D) secret
   E) bad

7. It was *customary* for him to be at work on time. *Customary* means most nearly
   A) curious
   B) necessary
   C) difficult
   D) common
   E) important

8. An attempt was made to *unite* the groups. *Unite* means most nearly
   A) improve
   B) serve
   C) uphold
   D) advise
   E) combine

9. The leader *defended* his followers. *Defended* means most nearly
   A) praised
   B) liked
   C) informed
   D) protected
   E) delayed

10. The *aim* of the employees is to do their work well. *Aim* means most nearly
    A) hope
    B) purpose
    C) duty
    D) promise
    E) idea

11. The workers will *assemble* the sacks of mail before loading them on the truck. *Assemble* means most nearly
    A) bring together
    B) examine carefully
    C) locate
    D) fill
    E) mark

12. The mayor of the city sent a letter to each of the *merchants*. *Merchants* means most nearly
    A) producers
    B) advertisers
    C) bankers
    D) executives
    E) storekeepers

13. The clerk was *compelled* to concentrate on his job. *Compelled* means most nearly
    A) tempted
    B) persuaded
    C) forced
    D) unable
    E) content

14. The clerk *extended* his vacation. *Extended* means most nearly
    A) limited
    B) deserved
    C) enjoyed
    D) lengthened
    E) started

15. The *territory* is too large to see in one day. *Territory* means most nearly
    A) swamp
    B) region
    C) city
    D) beach
    E) terminal

16. The technicians *created* a new machine. *Created* means most nearly
    A) planned
    B) copied
    C) invented
    D) tried
    E) replaced

17. The *mended* mail sacks will be delivered. *Mended* means most nearly
    A) repaired
    B) torn
    C) clean
    D) labelled
    E) tied

18. The new post office building is *huge*. *Huge* means most nearly
    A) ugly
    B) tall
    C) sturdy
    D) immense
    E) narrow

19. He was asked to *mingle* with the other guests. *Mingle* means most nearly
    A) consult
    B) visit
    C) sing
    D) mix
    E) dance

20. The director of the program is *likewise* chairman of the committee. *Likewise* means most nearly
    A) also
    B) often
    C) thus
    D) however
    E) meanwhile

21. Doctors are determined to *conquer* the disease. *Conquer* means most nearly
    A) study
    B) fight
    C) overcome
    D) eliminate
    E) trace

22. The machine was *designed* for stamping envelopes. *Designed* means most nearly
    A) fine
    B) used
    C) essential
    D) approved
    E) intended

23. He *mourned* the loss of his friend. *Mourned* means most nearly
    A) resented
    B) grieved
    C) remembered
    D) avenged
    E) faced

24. The meeting will take place at the *usual* time. *Usual* means most nearly
    A) proper
    B) old
    C) customary
    D) best
    E) earliest

25. The employee was given *distinct* instructions. *Distinct* means most nearly
    A) clear
    B) short
    C) new
    D) regular
    E) loud

26. The worker will *bind* the pages together. *Bind* means most nearly
    A) press
    B) receive
    C) make
    D) return
    E) fasten

27. He *startled* the person standing next to him. *Startled* means most nearly
    A) alarmed
    B) touched
    C) scolded
    D) reassured
    E) avoided

28. He *deceived* them by claiming to be rich. *Deceived* means most nearly
    A) favored
    B) tricked
    C) impressed
    D) imitated
    E) angered

29. The flood brought *distress* to many families. *Distress* means most nearly
    A) shock
    B) illness
    C) suffering
    D) risk
    E) hunger

30. Some of the statements made at the meeting were *absurd*. *Absurd* means most nearly
    A) clever
    B) original
    C) careless
    D) foolish
    E) serious

31. The supervisor *implied* that the schedule would be changed. *Implied* means most nearly
    A) acknowledged
    B) imagined
    C) suggested
    D) predicted
    E) insisted

32. Each person works to earn his own *livelihood*. *Livelihood* means most nearly
    A) salary
    B) employment
    C) fortune
    D) education
    E) maintenance

If you finish before the time is up, check your answers to this part. Do not go to any other part.

CORRECT ANSWERS FOR MAIL HANDLER TEST

Following Oral Directions Booklet

Important! This booklet is to be read aloud to you; do not read it to yourself.

Instructions to the person who will read the directions

The sample questions are to be read first. All the answers to the samples should be marked on the Sample Answer Sheet.

These instructions should be read at about 80 words per minute. You should practice reading the material in the box until you can do it in exactly 1 minute. This will give you a feel for the way you should read the test material.

> Look at line 20 in your work booklet. There are two circles and two boxes of different sizes with numbers in them. If 7 is less than 3 and if 2 is smaller than 4, write a G in the larger circle. Otherwise write a B as in baker in the smaller box. Now on your code sheet, darken the space for the number-letter combination in the box or circle.

You should read this test aloud before you read it to the person taking the test, in order to acquaint yourself with the procedure and the desired rate of reading.

You should read slowly but at a natural pace. That is, you should not space the words so that there are unnaturally long pauses between them. The instruction "Pause slightly" indicates only enough time to take a breath. The other instructions for pauses give the recommended length of pauses. If possible use a watch with a second hand.

All the material in this booklet except the words in parentheses, starting where indicated below, is to be read aloud.

START READING BELOW:

On the job you will have to listen to directions and then do what you have been told to do. In this test, I will read instructions to you. Try to understand them as I read them; I cannot repeat them. Do not ask questions from now until the end of the test.

You are to write in your booklet according to the directions that I'll read to you. After each set of instructions, I will give you time to mark your answers on an answer sheet.

For each answer you will darken the space for a number-letter combination. When you finish the test, you should have no more than one box marked for each number. If more than one box is marked for a number, it will be counted as an error.

On the job, you won't have to deal with pictures, numbers, and letters like those in the test, but you will have to listen to instructions, and follow them. We are using this test to see how well you can follow instructions.

Before we do the test itself, we will do some samples. Open your book to page 5.

Look at the samples. Sample 1 has a number and a line beside it. On the line write an A. (Pause 2 seconds.) Now on the Sample Answer Sheet on page 5 of your test booklet, find number 7 (pause 2 seconds) and darken the box for the letter you just wrote on the line. (Pause 2 seconds.)

Look at Sample 2. (Pause slightly.) Draw a line under the second number in the line. (Pause 2 seconds.) Now on the Sample Answer Sheet find the number under which you just drew a line and darken box B as in baker for that number. (Pause 5 seconds.)

Now look at the five circles in the third line of samples. (Pause slightly.) Each circle has a number and a line in it. Write a D as in dog on the blank in the last circle. (Pause 2 seconds.) Now on the Sample Answer Sheet darken the space for the number-letter combination that is in the circle you just wrote in. (Pause 5 seconds.)

Now look at the five boxes in Sample 4. Each box has a line and a letter. (Pause slightly.) In the first box write the answer to this question: How many pennies are there in a dime? (Pause 2 seconds.) Now on the Sample Answer Sheet darken the space for the number-letter combination that is in the box you just wrote in. (Pause 5 seconds.)

Now look at the Sample Answer Sheet. (Pause slightly.) You should have darkened spaces 2B, 6D, 7A, and 10A on the Sample Answer Sheet. Did you darken any other space? (Pause slightly.)

You are to mark your test booklet according to the instructions that I'll read to you. After each set of instructions, I'll give you time to record your answers on your regular answer sheet.

In this test, I will read instructions to you. Try to understand them as I read them; I cannot repeat them. Do not ask any questions from now on.

If, when you go to darken a box for a number, you find that you have already darkened another box for that number, either erase the first mark and darken the box for the new combination or let the first mark stay and do not darken a box for the new combination. When you finish, you should have no more than one box darkened for each number.

Turn to the next page in your test booklet.

You will use Part B of your answer sheet for this part of the test.

Look at line 1 in your test booklet. (Pause slightly.) Draw a line under the fourth number in the line. (Pause 2 seconds.) Now, on your answer sheet, find the number under which just drew the line and darken box A for that number. (Pause 5 seconds.)

Look at the letters in line 2 in your test booklet. (Pause slightly.) Draw a line under the fifth letter in the line. Now on your answer sheet find number 15 (pause 2 seconds) and darken the box for the letter under which you drew a line. (Pause 5 seconds.)

Look at the letters in line 2 in your test booklet again. (Pause slightly.) Now draw two lines under the third letter in the line. (Pause 2 seconds.) Now, on your answer sheet, find number 21 (pause 2 seconds) and darken the box for the letter under which you drew two lines. (Pause 5 seconds.)

Look at line 3 in your test booklet. (Pause slightly.) Write an E in the last box. (Pause 2 seconds.) Now, on your answer sheet, find the number in that box and darken box E for that number. (Pause 5 seconds.)

Now look at line 3 again. (Pause slightly.) Write an A in the first box. (Pause 2 seconds.) Now, on your answer sheet, find the number in that box and darken box A for that number. (Pause 5 seconds.)

Look at line 4. The number in each circle is the number of packages in a mail sack. In the circle for the sack holding the largest number of packages, write a B as in baker. (Pause 2 seconds.) Now, on your answer sheet, darken the space for the number-letter combination that is in the circle you just wrote in. (Pause 5 seconds.)

Look at line 4 again. In the circle for the sack holding the smallest number of packages, write an E. (Pause 2 seconds.) Now, on your answer sheet, darken the space for the number-letter combination that is in the circle you just wrote in. (Pause 5 seconds.)

Look at the drawings on line 5 in your test booklet. The four boxes are trucks for carrying mail. (Pause slightly.) The truck with the highest number is to be loaded first. Write a B as in baker on the line beside the highest number. (Pause 2 seconds.) Now, on your answer sheet, darken the space for the number-letter combination that is in the box you just wrote in. (Pause 5 seconds.)

Look at line 6 in your test booklet. (Pause slightly.) Next to the middle number write the letter D as in dog. (Pause 2 seconds.) Now, on your answer sheet, find the space for the number beside which you wrote and darken box D as in dog. (Pause 5 seconds.)

Look at the five circles in line 7 in your test booklet. Write B as in baker on the blank in the second circle. (Pause 2 seconds.) Now, on your answer sheet, darken the space for the number-letter combination that is in the circle you just wrote in. (Pause 5 seconds.)

Now take your test booklet again and write C on the blank in the third circle on line 7. (Pause 2 seconds.) Now, on your answer sheet, darken the space for the number-letter combination that is in the circle you just wrote in. (Pause 5 seconds.)

Now look at line 8 in your test booklet. (Pause slightly.) Write an A on the line next to the right-hand number. (Pause 2 seconds.) Now, on your answer sheet, find the space for the number beside which you wrote and darken box A. (Pause 5 seconds.)

Look at line 9 in your test booklet. (Pause slightly.) Draw a line under every number that is more than 20 but less than 30. (Pause 12 seconds.) Now, on your answer sheet, for each number that you drew a line under, darken box C. (Pause 25 seconds.)

Look at line 10 in your test booklet. (Pause slightly.) Draw a line under every number that is more than 5 and less than 15. (Pause 10 seconds.) Now, on your answer sheet, for each number you drew a line under, darken box D as in dog. (Pause 25 seconds.)

Look at line 11 in your test booklet. (Pause slightly.) In each circle there is a time when the mail must leave. In the circle for the latest time, write on the line the last two figures of the time. (Pause 5 seconds.) Now, on your answer sheet, darken the space for the number-letter combination that is in the circle you just wrote in. (Pause 5 seconds.)

Turn to the next page of the test booklet. (Pause until page has been turned.) Look at the five boxes in line 12 in your test booklet. (Pause slightly.) If 6 is less than 3, put an E in the fourth box. (Pause slightly.) If 6 is not less than 3, put a B as in baker in the first box. (Pause 5 seconds.) Now, on your answer sheet, darken the space for the number-letter combination that is in the box you just wrote in. (Pause 5 seconds.)

Now look at line 13 in your test booklet. (Pause slightly.) There are 5 circles. Each circle has a letter. (Pause slightly.) In the second circle, write the answer to this question: Which of the following numbers is smallest: 32, 11, 22, 31, 16? (Pause 5 seconds.) Now, on your answer sheet, darken the space for the number-letter combination that is in the circle you just wrote in. (Pause 5 seconds.) In the third circle on the same line, write 28. (Pause 2 seconds.) Now, on your answer sheet, darken the space for the number-letter combination that is in the circle you just wrote in. (Pause 5 seconds.) In the fourth circle do nothing. In the fifth circle write the answer to this question: How many months are there in a year? (Pause 2 seconds.) Now, on your answer sheet, darken the space for the number-letter combination that is in the circle you just wrote in. (Pause 5 seconds.)

Look at line 14 in your test booklet. (Pause slightly.) There are two circles and two boxes of different sizes with numbers in them. (Pause slightly.) If 2 is smaller than 4 and if 7 is less than 3, write A in the larger circle. (Pause slightly.) Otherwise write B as in baker in the smaller box. (Pause 2 seconds.) Now, on your answer sheet, darken the space for the number-letter combination in the box or circle in which you just wrote. (Pause 5 seconds.)

Look at the boxes and words in line 15 in your test booklet. (Pause slightly.) Write the second letter of the first word in the third box. (Pause 2 seconds.) Write the first letter of the second word in the first box. (Pause 2 seconds.) Write the first letter of the third word in the second box. (Pause 2 seconds.) Now on your answer sheet, darken the spaces for the number-letter combinations that are in the three boxes you just wrote in. (Pause 10 seconds.)

Look at line 16 in your test booklet. (Pause slightly.) Draw a line under every "O" in the line. (Pause 5 seconds.) Count the number of lines that you have drawn, subtract 2, and write that number at the end of the line. (Pause 5 seconds.) Now, on your answer sheet, find that number and darken space D as in dog for that number. (Pause 5 seconds.)

Look at line 17 in your test booklet. (Pause slightly.) If the number in the left-hand circle is smaller than the number in the right-hand circle, add 2 to the number in the left-hand circle, and change the number in that circle to this number. (Pause 8 seconds.) Then write B as in baker next to the new number. (Pause slightly.) Otherwise write E next to the number in the smaller box. (Pause 3 seconds.) Then, on your answer sheet, darken the space for the number-letter combination that is in the box or circle you just wrote in. (Pause 5 seconds.)

Look at line 18 in your test booklet. (Pause slightly.) If in a year January comes before February, write A in the box with the smallest number. (Pause slightly.) If it does not, write C in the box with the largest number. (Pause 3 seconds.) Now, on your answer sheet, darken the space for the number-letter combination that is in the box you just wrote in. (Pause 5 seconds.)

Now look at line 19 in your test booklet. (Pause slightly.) Mail for Detroit and Hartford is to be put in box 3. (Pause slightly.) Mail for Cleveland and St. Louis is to be put in box 26. (Pause slightly.) Write C in the box in which you put mail for St. Louis. Now, on your answer sheet, darken the space for the number-letter combination that is in the box you just wrote in. (Pause 5 seconds.)

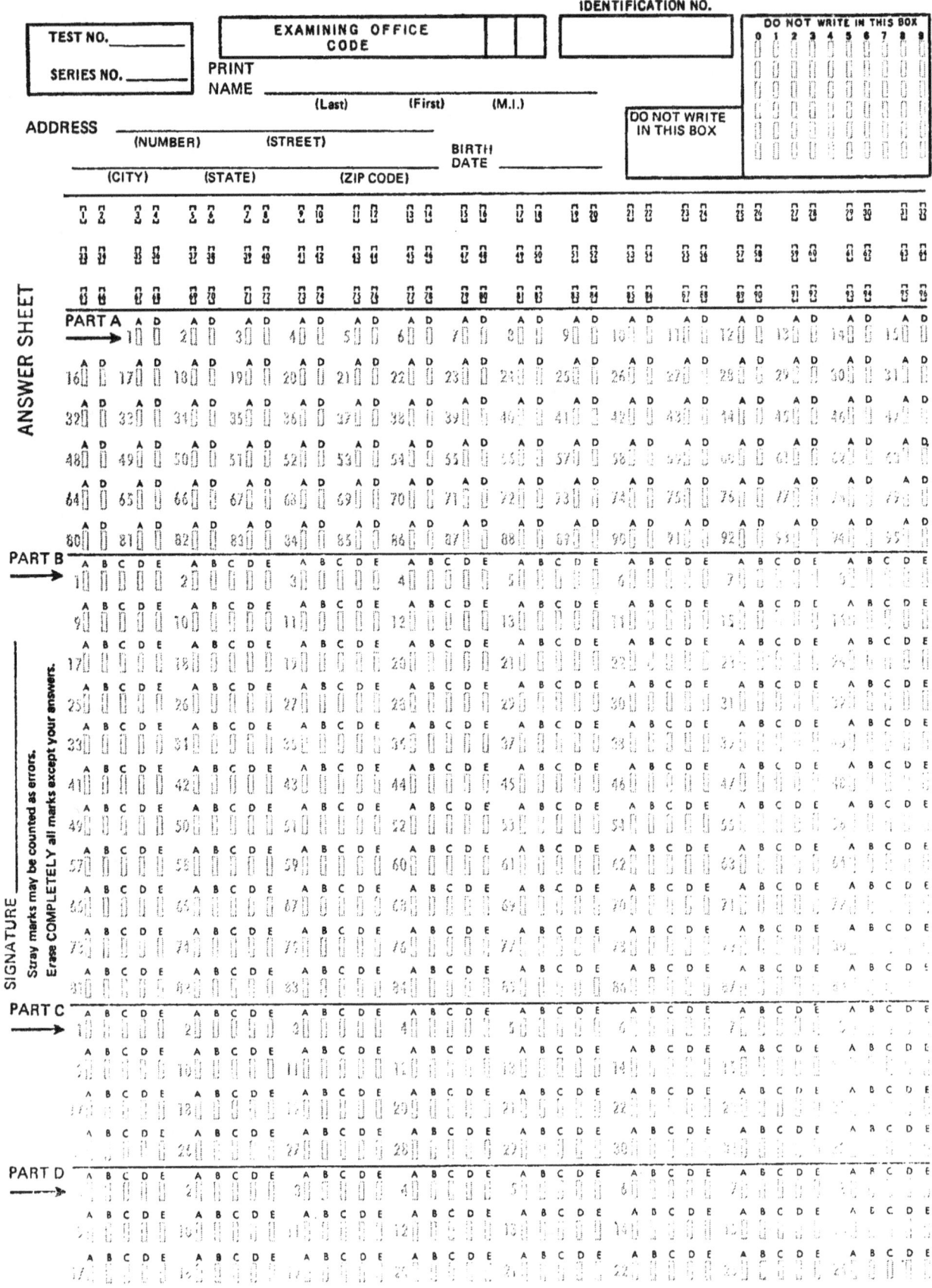

Address Checking

DESCRIPTION OF THE TEST AND SAMPLE QUESTIONS

Every member of the Postal work force is responsible for seeing that every letter reaches the right address. If one worker makes an error in reading an address, it can cause a serious delay in getting the letter to where it is supposed to go.

Both the Clerk-Carrier and Mail Handler examinations include tests of address checking. The test in the Clerk-Carrier examination is harder than the one in the Mail Handler examination. The Mail Handler test has only names of cities and states with some zip codes, while the Clerk-Carrier test has street addresses also.

Can you spot whether or not two addresses are alike or different? It is as easy as that. But how fast can you do it accurately? Look at the sample questions below. Each question consists of a pair of addresses like this—

762 W 18th St   762 W 18th St
   Are they Alike or Different? They are exactly Alike.
9486 Hillsdale Rd   9489 Hillsdale Rd
   Alike or Different? They are Different. Do you see why?
1242 RegalSt   1242 Regel St
   Alike or Different?

Remember that this test measures both speed and accuracy. So work as fast as you can without making any mistakes. Have a friend time you while you are working on the practice tests—you may find that you get faster as you become used to this type of question.

Hints for Answering Address-Checking Questions
- Do not spend too much time on any one question.
- The difference may not be noticeable at first, so be sure to check
  —all numbers (are they alike and in the same order or are they different)
  —abbreviations, such as St, Rd, NW, N Y (are they alike or are they different)
  —spellings of street, city, and state names
- Do not get nervous about the time limit. (In the official test no one is expected to do all the questions in the time allowed.)
- Make sure that you have marked the correct box for each question.

Address Checking—Sample Questions

Starting now, if the two addresses are ALIKE darken box A on the Sample Answer Sheet below. If the two addresses are DIFFERENT in any way darken box D. Answer every question.

1 ... 239 Windell Ave   239 Windell Ave
   Alike or Different? Alike. Mark space A for question 1.
2 ... 4667 Edgeworth Rd   4677 Edgeworth Rd
   Alike or Different? Different. Mark space D for question 2.
3 ... 2661 Kennel St SE   2661 Kennel St SW
4 ... 3709 Columbine St   3707 Columbine St
5 ... 969 W 14th St NW   969 W 14th St NW
6 ... 4439 Frederick Pkwy   4439 Frederick Pkwy
7 ... 77 Summers St   77 Summers St
8 ... 828 N Franklin Pl   828 S Franklin Pl

Check your answers with the correct answers. If you have any wrong answers, be sure you see why before you go on.

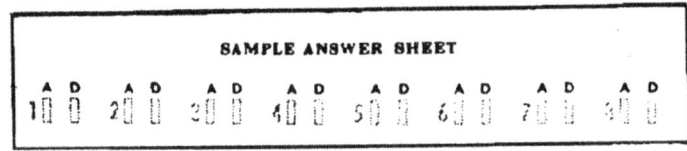

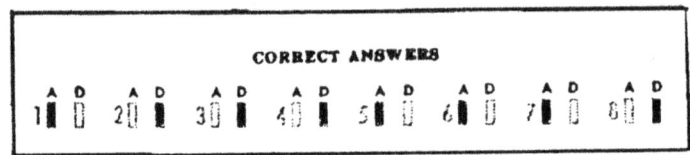

The addresses in the Practice Tests are like the ones you will have to check in the examinations. The ones in Practice Test 1 are like the ones in the Mail Handler examination. Work as fast as you can, but be careful because you will lose points for making mistakes. Be sure to take no more than the correct time for each test. Check your answers with the answers at the end of each test.

Now turn the page and take the first Practice Test.

ADDRESS CHECKING—PRACTICE TEST 1

Work exactly *3 minutes.* No more. No less. If you finish before the 3 minutes are up, go over your answers again. Be sure to mark your answers on the Sample Answer Sheet on the next page.

1 ...	Purdin Mo	Purdon Mo
2 ...	Hobart Ind 46342	Hobart Ind 46342
3 ...	Kuna Idaho	Kuna Idaho
4 ...	Janesville Calif 96114	Janesville Calif 96119
5 ...	Sioux Falls S Dak	Sioux Falls S Dak
6 ...	Homewood Miss	Homewood Miss
7 ...	Kaweah Calif	Kawaeh Calif
8 ...	Unionport Ohio	Unionport Ohio
9 ...	Meyersdale Pa	Meyersdale Va
10 ...	Coquille Oreg 97423	Coqville Oreg 97423
11 ...	Milan Wis	Milam Wis
12 ...	Prospect Ky	Prospect Ky
13 ...	Cloversville N Y	Cloverville N Y
14 ...	Locate Mont 59340	Locate Mont 59340
15 ...	Bozman Md	Bozeman Md
16 ...	Orient Ill	Orient Ill
17 ...	Yosemite Ky 42566	Yosemite Ky 42566
18 ...	Camden Miss 39045	Camden Miss 39054
19 ...	Bennington Vt	Bennington Vt
20 ...	La Farge Wis	La Farge Wis
21 ...	Fairfield N Y	Fairfield N C
22 ...	Wynot Nebr	Wynot Nebr
23 ...	Arona Pa	Aroda Pa
24 ...	Thurman N C 28683	Thurmond N C 28683
25 ...	Zenda Kans	Zenba Kans
26 ...	Pike N H	Pike N H
27 ...	Gorst Wash 98337	Gorst Wash 98837
28 ...	Joiner Ark	Joiner Ark
29 ...	Normangee Tex	Normangee Tex
30 ...	Toccoa Ga	Tococa Ga
31 ...	Small Point Maine 04567	Small Point Maine 04567
32 ...	Eagan Tenn	Eagar Tenn
33 ...	Belfield N Dak	Belford N Dak
34 ...	De Ridder La 70634	De Ridder La 70634
35 ...	Van Meter Iowa	Van Meter Iowa
36 ...	Valparaiso Fla	Valparaiso Ind
37 ...	Souris N Dak	Souris N Dak
38 ...	Robbinston Maine	Robbinstown Maine
39 ...	Dawes W Va 25054	Dawes W Va 25054
40 ...	Goltry Okla	Goltrey Okla

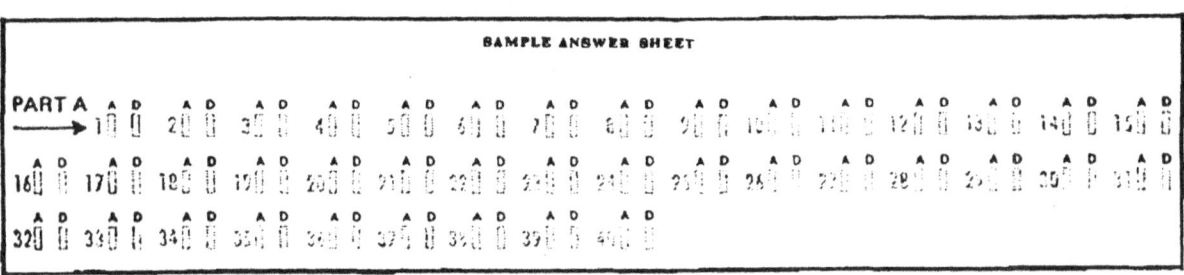

Now check your answers by comparing your answers with the correct answers shown below.

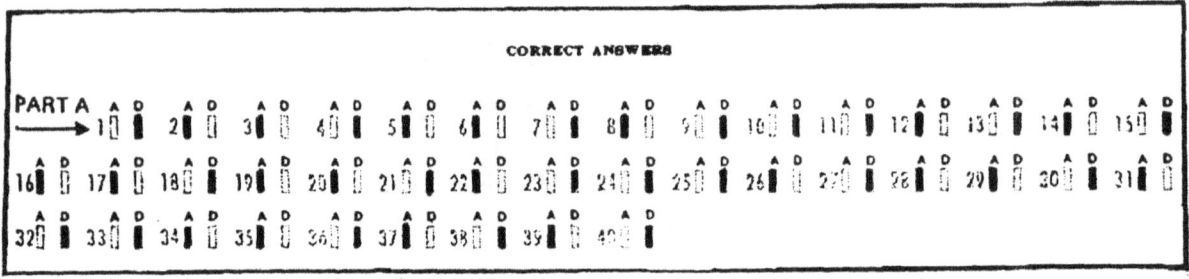

Count how many you got right, and write that number on this line ─────────────────────────► Number Right ─────

Now count how many you got wrong, and write that number on this line ─────────────────────────► Number Wrong ═════

Subtract the Number Wrong from the Number Right and write the Difference on this line ─────────────────► Total Score ─────

Meaning of Test Score

If your Total Score is *26 or more,* you have a Good score.
If your Total Score is from *16 to 25,* you have a Fair score.
If your Total Score is *15 or less,* you are not doing too well.
   You may be going too slowly, or you may be making too many mistakes. You need more practice.

ADDRESS CHECKING—PRACTICE TEST 2

These addresses are a little harder.

Remember to work as fast as you can but be careful. Work exactly *3 minutes*. No more. No less. If you finish before the 3 minutes are up, go over your answers again. Be sure to mark your answers on the Sample Answer Sheet on the next page.

1 ...	7961 Eastern Ave SE	7961 Eastern Ave SE
2 ...	3809 20th Rd N	3309 20th Rd N
3 ...	Smicksburg Pa	Smithsburg Pa
4 ...	Sherman Conn	Sherman Conn
5 ...	Richland Ga	Richland La
6 ...	8520 Leesburg Pike SE	8520 Leesburg Pike SE
7 ...	Genevia Ark	Geneva Ark
8 ...	104 W Jefferson St	104 W Jefferson St
9 ...	Meandor WVa	Meander W Va
10 ...	6327 W Mari Ct	6327 W Mari Ct
11 ...	3191 Draper Dr SE	3191 Draper Dr SW
12 ...	1415 W Green Spring Rd	1415 W Green Spring Rd
13 ...	Parr Ind	Parr Ind
14 ...	East Falmouth Mass 02536	East Falmouth Miss 02536
15 ...	3016 N St NW	3016 M St NW
16 ...	Yukon Mo	Yukon Mo
17 ...	7057 Brookfield Plaza	7057 Brookfield Plaza
18 ...	Bethel Ohio 45106	Bethel Ohio 45106
19 ...	Littleton N H	Littleton N C
20 ...	8909 Bowie Dr	8909 Bowie Dr
21 ...	Colmar I11	Colmar I11
22 ...	784 Matthews Dr NE	784 Matthews Dr NE
23 ...	2923 John Marshall Dr	2932 John Marshall Dr
24 ...	6023 Woodmont Rd	6023 Woodmount Rd
25 ...	Nolan Tex	Noland Tex
26 ...	342 E Lincolnia Rd	342 E Lincolnia Dr
27 ...	Jane Calif	Jane Calif
28 ...	4921 Seminary Rd	4912 Seminary Rd
29 ...	Ulmers S C	Ullmers S C
30 ...	4804 Montgomery Lane SW	4804 Montgomery Lane SW
31 ...	210 E Fairfax Dr	210 W Fairfax Dr
32 ...	Hanapepe Hawaii	Hanapepe Hawaii
33 ...	450 La Calle del Punto	450 La Calle del Punto
34 ...	Walland Tenn 37886	Walland Tenn 37836
35 ...	Villamont Va	Villamont Va
36 ...	4102 Georgia Ave NW	4102 Georgia Rd NW
37 ...	Aroch Oreg	Aroch Oreg
38 ...	6531 N Walton Ave	6531 N Waldon Ave
39 ...	Jeff Ky	Jeff Ky
40 ...	Delphos Iowa	Delphis Iowa

SAMPLE ANSWER SHEET

PART A — [answer grid, items 1–40, with A/D bubble marks]

Now check your answers by comparing your answers with the correct answers shown below.

CORRECT ANSWERS

PART A — [answer key grid, items 1–40, with A/D bubble marks]

Count how many you got right, and write that number on this line ──────────────▶ Number Right ─────

Now count how many you got wrong, and write that number on this line ──────────────▶ Number Wrong ─────

Subtract the Number Wrong from the Number Right and write the Difference on this line ──────────────▶ Total Score ─────

Meaning of Test Score

If your Total Score is *26 or more,* you have a Good score.

If your Total Score is from *16 to 25,* you have a Fair score.

If your Total Score is *15 or less,* you are not doing too well.

You may be going too slowly, or you may be making too many mistakes. You need more practice.

ADDRESS CHECKING-PRACTICE TEST 3

These addresses are exactly like the ones in the Clerk-Carrier examination. Even if you don't plan to take the Clerk-Carrier examination, this is good practice for the Mail Handler one. Work as fast as you can without making too many errors. Work exactly *3 minutes*. No more. No less. If you finish before the 3 minutes are up, go over your answers again. Mark your answers on the Sample Answer Sheet on the next page.

1 ...	2134 S 20th St	2134 S 20th St
2 ...	4608 N Warnock St	4806 N Warnock St
3 ...	1202 W Girard Dr	1202 W Girard Rd
4 ...	3120 S Harcourt St	3120 S Harcourt St
5 ...	4618 W Addison St	4618 E Addison St
6 ...	Sessums Miss	Sessoms Miss
7 ...	6425 N Delancey	6425 N Delancey
8 ...	5407 Columbia Rd	5407 Columbia Rd
9 ...	2106 Southern Ave	2106 Southern Ave
10 ...	Highfalls N C 27259	Highlands NC 27259
11 ...	2873 Pershing Dr	2873 Pershing Dr
12 ...	1329 N H Ave NW	1329 N J Ave NW
13 ...	1316 N Quinn St	1316 N Quinn St
14 ...	7507 Wyngate Dr	7505 Wyngate Dr
15 ...	2918 Colesville Rd	2918 Colesvale Rd
16 ...	2071 E Belvedere Dr	2071 E Belvedere Dr
17 ...	Palmer Wash	Palmer Mich
18 ...	2106 16th St SW	2106 16th St SW
19 ...	2207 Markland Ave	2207 Markham Ave
20 ...	5345 16th St SW	5345 16th St SE
21 ...	239 Summit Pl NE	239 Summit Pl NE
22 ...	152 Continental Pkwy	152 Continental Blvd
23 ...	8092 13th Rd S	8029 13th Rd S
24 ...	3906 Queensbury Rd	3906 Queensbury Rd
25 ...	4719 Linnean Ave NW	4719 Linnean Ave NE
26 ...	Bradford Me	Bradley Me
27 ...	Parrott Ga 31777	Parrott Ga 31177
28 ...	4312 Lowell Lane	4312 Lowell Lane
29 ...	6929 W 135th Place	6929 W 135th Plaza
30 ...	5143 Somerset Cir	5143 Somerset Cir
31 ...	8501 Kennedy St	8501 Kennedy St
32 ...	2164 E McLean Ave	2164 E McLean Ave
33 ...	7186 E St NW	7186 F St NW
34 ...	2121 Beechcrest Rd	2121 Beechcroft Rd
35 ...	3609 E Montrose St	3609 E Montrose St
36 ...	324 S Alvadero St	324 S Alverado St
37 ...	2908 Plaza de las Estrellas	2908 Plaza de las Estrellas
38 ...	223 Great Falls Rd SE	223 Great Falls Dr SE
39 ...	Kelton S C 29354	Kelton S C 29354
40 ...	3201 Landover Rd	3201 Landover Rd

```
                              SAMPLE ANSWER SHEET
    PART A  A D   A D   A D   A D   A D   A D   A D   A D   A D   A D   A D   A D   A D   A D   A D
    ──►
           A D   A D   A D   A D   A D   A D   A D   A D   A D   A D   A D   A D   A D   A D   A D
           16    17    18    19    20    21    22    23    24    25    26    27    28    29    30
           A D   A D   A D   A D   A D   A D   A D   A D   A D
           32    33    34    35    36    37    38    39    40
```

Now check your answers by comparing your answers with the correct answers shown below.

```
                              CORRECT ANSWERS
    PART A  A D   A D   A D   A D   A D   A D   A D   A D   A D   A D   A D   A D   A D   A D   A D
    ──► 1     2     3     4     5     6     7     8     9     10    11    12    13    14    15
           A D   A D   A D   A D   A D   A D   A D   A D   A D   A D   A D   A D   A D   A D   A D
           16    17    18    19    20    21    22    23    24    25    26    27    28    29    30
           A D   A D   A D   A D   A D   A D   A D   A D   A D
           32    33    34    35    36    37    38    39    40
```

Count how many you got right, and write that number on this
line ─────────────────────────────────► Number Right ─────

Now count how many you got wrong, and write that number on
this line ───────────────────────────► Number Wrong ─────

Subtract the Number Wrong from the Number Right and write
the Difference on this line ─────────────► Total Score ─────

Meaning of Test Score.
    If your Total Score is *26 or more,* you have a Good score.
    If your Total Score is from *16 to 25,* you have a Fair score.
    If your Total Score is *15 or less,* you are not doing too well.
        You may be going too slowly, or you may be making too many mistakes. You need more practice.

ADDRESS CHECKING
EXAMINATION SECTION
TEST 1

DIRECTIONS: The following test contains 60 questions to be completed in 11 minutes. The two lists below—the correct list on the left and the list to be checked on the right—are to be compared quickly and accurately in that time. Mark your answer A, B, C or D based on the following information:
Mark "A" if the two items are exactly the same (no errors)
Mark "B" if there is an error in the address only
Mark "C" if there is an error in the ZIP code only
Mark "D" if there are errors in both the address and ZIP code
PRINT THE LETTER OF THE CORRECT ANSWER IN THE SPACE AT THE RIGHT.

	CORRECT LIST		LIST TO BE CHECKED		
1.	149 Market St. Purdin, MO	64674	149 Market St. Purdin, MO	64674	1._____
2.	1212 Jeremy Dr. Hobart, IN	46342	1212 Jeremy Dr. Hobart, IN	46432	2._____
3.	39 Union Pkwy. Kuna, ID	83634	39 Union Pkwy. Kuna, ID	83684	3._____
4.	1001 Azalea Blvd. Janesville, CA	96114	1011 Azalea Blvd. Janesville, CA	96119	4._____
5.	991 Rockaway Rd. Sioux Falls, SD	57101	991 Rockaway Rd. Sioux Falls, SD	57101	5._____
6.	75 Gorton St. Homewood, PA	15208	75 Gordon St. Homewood, PA	15208	6._____
7.	154 Kenmore Rd. Kaweah, CA	93237	154 Kenmore Rd. Kawaeh, CA	93237	7._____
8.	501 Flower Rd. Unionport, OH	43910	501 Flower Rd. Unionsport, OH	43910	8._____
9.	198 South Brush Dr. Meyersdale, PA	15552	198 South Brush Dr. Meyersdale, PA	15552	9._____
10.	2109 E. 161st St. Coquille, OR	97423	2109 E. 161st St. Coquille, OR	97432	10._____
11.	331 McDugan Blvd. Milan, WI	54411	331 MacDugan Blvd. Milan, WI	54441	11._____
12.	239 Ellenville St. Prospect, KY	40059	239 Ellenville St. Prospect, NY	40099	12._____

13. 117 Arrow Way Gloversville, NY	12078	117 Arrow Way Gloversville, NY	12078	13._____
14. 226 Bowery Rd. Locate, MT	59340	226 Bowery Rd. Locate, MT	59340	14._____
15. 440 West Shore Dr. Bozman, MD	21612	440 West Shore Dr. Bozeman, MD	21612	15._____
16. 5501 Parker St. Orient, IL	62874	5501 Parker St. Orient, IL	62814	16._____
17. 11 Burke Blvd. Yosemite, KY	42566	11 Burke Blvd. Yosemite, KY	42556	17._____
18. 912 Croxley St. Camden, MS	39045	912 Croxley St. Camden, MS	39045	18._____
19. 54 Maple La. Bennington, VT	05201	54 Maple La. Bennington, VT	05201	19._____
20. 101 Badger Blvd. La Farge, WI	54639	101 Badger Blvd. Le Farge, WI	54633	20._____
21. 201 Westminster Rd. Fairfield, NC	27826	201 Eastminster Rd. Fairfield, NC	27826	21._____
22. 315 Frazier Pl. Wynot, NE	68792	315 Frazier Pl. Wynot, NE	68792	22._____
23. 808 Appleton St. Arona, PA	15617	808 Appleton St. Arona, PA	15677	23._____
24. 2262 Blackberry Dr. Thurmond, NC	28683	2262 Blackberry Dr. Thurmond, NC	28633	24._____
25. 369 Jayhawk Pkwy. Zenda, KS	67159	369 Jayhawk Pkwy. Zenba, KS	67159	25._____
26. 117 Plateau St. Pike, NH	03780	117 Plateau Rd. Pike, NH	03780	26._____
27. 20 Forest Ave. Gorst, WA	98337	20 Forest Ave. Gorst, WA	98337	27._____
28. 400 Littleview Pkwy. Joiner, AR	72350	400 Littleview Pkwy. Joiner, AZ	72530	28._____
29. 211 Fields St. Normangee, TX	77871	211 Fields St. Normangee, TX	77871	29._____

30. 47 Pollack Dr. Toccoa, GA	30577	47 Pollack Dr. Tococa, GA	30057	30._____
31. 4884 Harborport St. Small Point, ME	04567	4884 Harborport St. Small Point, ME	04567	31._____
32. 25 Frank St. Eagan, TN	37730	25 Frank St. Eagar, TN	37330	32._____
33. 38 Lakeview Terr. Belfield, ND	58622	38 Lakeview Terr. Belfield, ND	53622	33._____
34. 1024 Saban St. De Ridder, LA	70634	1024 Saban St. De Ridder, LA	70634	34._____
35. 206 Banks Blvd. Van Meter, IA	50261	206 Banks Blvd. Van Meter, IA	50261	35._____
36. 624 Bryce La. Valparaiso, FL	32580	624 Bryce La. Valparaiso, FL	32580	36._____
37. 11 Hemingway St. Souris, ND	58783	11 Hemmingway St. Souris, ND	58783	37._____
38. 88 Pine St. Robbinston, ME	04671	88 Pine St. Robbinston, ME	04671	38._____
39. 227 Gansey Rd. Dawes, WV	25054	227 Gansey Rd. Dawes, WV	25854	39._____
40. 187 Clayton Ct. Goltry, OK	73739	187 Clayton St. Goltry, OK	73789	40._____
41. 7961 Eastern Ave. SE Jacksonville, FL	32209	7961 Eastern Ave. SE Jacksonville, FL	32209	41._____
42. 3809 20th Rd. Manhattan, KS	66503	3809 20th Rd. Manhattan, NY	66503	42._____
43. 177 Andrews Cir. Smicksburg, PA	16256	177 Andrews Cir. Smicksburg, PA	16266	43._____
44. 90 Birdstone Sq. Sherman, CT	06784	90 Birdstone St. Sherman, CT	06734	44._____
45. 4717 Greene St. Richland, GA	31825	4717 Greene St. Richland, GA	31825	45._____
46. 8520 Leesburg Pike SE Boise, ID	83706	8520 Leesburg Pike SE Boise, ID	83706	46._____

47. 919 Little Bay Pkwy. 71840   919 Little Bay Pkwy. 71840   47._____
    Genoa, AR   Genoa, AR

48. 104 W. Jefferson St. 13210   140 W. Jefferson St. 13012   48._____
    Syracuse, NY   Syracuse, NY

49. 77 Tottenham Pl.   26283   77 Tottenham Pl.   26283   49._____
    Montrose, WV   Montross, WV

50. 6327 W. Mari Ct.   92129   6237 W. Mari Ct.   92129   50._____
    San Diego, CA   San Diego, CA

51. 3191 Draper Dr.   11791   3191 Draper Dr.   11771   51._____
    Syosset, NY   Syosset, NY

52. 1415 Green Spring Rd. 32132   1415 Green Spring Rd. 32132   52._____
    Edgewater, FL   Edgewater, FL

53. 1231 Davis Blvd.   46391   1231 Davis Blvd.   46991   53._____
    Otis, IN   Ottis, IN

54. 820 McMurphy Ave.   02536   820 McMurphy Ave.   02536   54._____
    East Falmouth, MA   East Falmouth, MA

55. 3016 N St. NW   42001   3016 N St. NW   42001   55._____
    Paducah, KY   Paducah, KY

56. 220 Quinn St.   65589   220 Quinn St.   65589   56._____
    Yukon, MO   Yukon, MA

57. 7057 Brookfield Plaza 10025   7507 Brookfield Plaza 10025   57._____
    New York, NY   New York, NY

58. 900 Zwiegert Pl.   45106   900 Zwiegert Pl.   45706   58._____
    Bethel, OH   Bethel, OH

59. 450 Daly Blvd.   03561   450 Daly Blvd.   03561   59._____
    Littleton, NH   Littleton, NH

60. 8909 Bowie Dr.   60087   8909 Bowie Dr.   60087   60._____
    Waukegan, IL   Waukegan, IL

KEY (CORRECT ANSWERS)

1. A	11. D	21. B	31. A	41. A	51. C
2. C	12. D	22. A	32. D	42. B	52. A
3. C	13. A	23. C	33. C	43. C	53. D
4. D	14. A	24. C	34. A	44. D	54. A
5. A	15. B	25. B	35. A	45. A	55. A
6. B	16. C	26. B	36. A	46. A	56. B
7. B	17. C	27. A	37. B	47. A	57. B
8. B	18. A	28. D	38. A	48. D	58. C
9. A	19. A	29. A	39. C	49. B	59. A
10. C	20. D	30. D	40. D	50. B	60. A

TEST 2

DIRECTIONS: The following test contains 60 questions to be completed in 11 minutes. The two lists below—the correct list on the left and the list to be checked on the right—are to be compared quickly and accurately in that time. Mark your answer A, B, C or D based on the following information:
Mark "A" if the two items are exactly the same (no errors)
Mark "B" if there is an error in the address only
Mark "C" if there is an error in the ZIP code only
Mark "D" if there are errors in both the address and ZIP code
PRINT THE LETTER OF THE CORRECT ANSWER IN THE SPACE AT THE RIGHT.

	CORRECT LIST		LIST TO BE CHECKED		
1.	919 Hannigan Blvd. Colmar, IL	62367	919 Hannigan Blvd. Colmar, IL	62367	1.____
2.	784 Matthews Dr. NE Ocala, FL	34476	784 Matthews Dr. Ocala, FL	34776	2.____
3.	2923 John Marshall Dr. Los Angeles, CA	90018	2923 John Marshall Dr. Los Angeles, CA	90008	3.____
4.	6023 Woodmont Rd. Kennesaw, GA	30144	6023 Woodmont Rd. Kennesaw, GA	30144	4.____
5.	127 Wesker Dr. Nolan, TX	79537	127 Wesker Dr. Noland, TX	79537	5.____
6.	342 E. Lincolnia Rd. Leesville, LA	71446	342 E. Lincolnia Rd. Leesville, LA	71446	6.____
7.	201 Montego Dr. Jenner, CA	95450	201 Montego Rd. Jenner, CA	94540	7.____
8.	4921 Seminary Rd. Fairbanks, AK	99709	4921 Seminary Rd. Fairbanks, AK	97709	8.____
9.	310 Felton St. Ulmer, SC	29849	310 Felton St. Ullmer, SC	29349	9.____
10.	4804 Montgomery La. Scottsdale, AZ	85259	4804 Montgomery La. Scottsdale, AZ	85529	10.____
11.	210 E. Fairfax Dr. Athens, GA	30601	210 E. Fairfax Dr. Athens, GA	30601	11.____
12.	450 Pinestraw Rd. Hanapepe, HI	96716	450 Pinestraw Rd. Hanapepe, HI	96716	12.____
13.	450 La Calle del Punto Miami, FL	33174	450 La Calle del Punto Miami, FL	33114	13.____

14. 806 Brennan Ct. Walland, TN	37886	806 Brennan Ct. Walland, TN	37886	14._____
15. 380 Smoken Dr. Villamont, VA	24178	380 Smoken Dr. Villamont, VA	24178	15._____
16. 4102 Georgia Ave. Hollywood, MD	20636	4102 Georgia Ave. Hollywood, MO	20636	16._____
17. 2500 Sisslen St. Arock, OR	97902	2500 Sisslen St. Aroch, OR	97002	17._____
18. 6531 N. Walton Ave. Albany, NY	12222	6531 N. Walton Ave. Albany, NY	12222	18._____
19. 15 Kelly Ave. Jeff, KY	41751	15 Kelly Ave. Jeff, KY	41751	19._____
20. 7240 Avenue K Dyersville, IA	52040	7240 Avenue K Dyersville, IA	52070	20._____
21. 2134 S. 20th St. Tampa, FL	33614	2314 S. 20th St. Tampa, FL	33674	21._____
22. 4608 N. Warnock St. Goshen, IN	46526	4608 N. Warnock St. Gashen, IN	46256	22._____
23. 1202 Girard Dr. Glen Burnie, MD	21061	1202 Girard Dr. Glen Burnie, MD	21061	23._____
24. 3120 S. Harcourt St. Brighton, MI	48116	3120 S. Harcourt St. Brighton, MI	48116	24._____
25. 4618 W. Addison St. Chicago, IL	60613	4618 W. Addison St. Chicago, IL	60613	25._____
26. 909 Eastgate Blvd. Sessums, MS	39759	909 East Gate Blvd. Sessums, MS	39759	26._____
27. 6425 N. Delancey St. St. Paul, MN	55124	6425 N. Delancey St. St. Paul, MN	55124	27._____
28. 5407 Columbia Rd. Billings, MT	59101	5407 Columbia Rd. Billings, MT	59010	28._____
29. 2106 Southern Ave. Glendale, CA	91205	2106 Southern Ave. Glendale, CA	97205	29._____
30. 1045 Chass Ct. Highfalls, NC	27259	1045 Chass Ct. Highfalls, NC	27259	30._____

31.	2873 Pershing Dr. Montgomery, AL	36108	2873 Pershing Dr. Montgomery, AZ	36180	31._____
32.	1329 N.H. Ave. NW Brooklyn, NY	11229	1329 N.H. Ave. NW Brooklyn, NY	11229	32._____
33.	1316 N. Quinn St. Chapel Hill, NC	27514	1316 N. Quin St. Chapel Hill, NC	27514	33._____
34.	7507 Wyngate Dr. Rockville, RI	02873	7507 Wyngate Dr. Rockville, RI	02878	34._____
35.	2918 Colesville Rd. Broomall, PA	19008	2819 Colesville Rd. Broomall, PA	19908	35._____
36.	2071 E. Belvedere Dr. Belton, SC	29627	2071 E. Belvadere Dr. Belton, SC	29927	36._____
37.	400 Sackmon St. Walla Walla, WA	99362	400 Sackmon St. Walla Walla, WA	93962	37._____
38.	2106 16th St. SW Ada, OK	74820	2106 16th St. SW Ada, OK	74820	38._____
39.	2207 Markland Ave. Cleveland, TN	37311	2207 Markland Ave. Cleveland, TN	37311	39._____
40.	5345 Langerhans Dr. Smoot, WY	83126	5345 Langerhans Dr. Smoot, WY	83126	40._____
41.	239 Summit Pl. Odessa, TX	79760	239 Summit Pl. Odessa, TN	79760	41._____
42.	152 Continental Pkwy. Reno, NV	89511	152 Continental Pkwy. Reno, NV	89511	42._____
43.	8092 13th Rd. S Alderson, WV	24910	8092 13th Rd. S Alderson, WV	24810	43._____
44.	3906 Queensbury Rd. Cincinnati, OH	45204	3906 Queensbury Rd. Cincinnati, OH	45004	44._____
45.	4719 Linnean Ave. Dalton, MA	01226	4719 Linnean Ave. Dallton, MA	00226	45._____
46.	5151 Vilma Dr. Bradford, ME	04410	5151 Vilma Dr. Bradford, ME	04410	46._____
47.	153 Abreu Ct. Parrott, GA	31777	153 Abreu St. Parrott, GA	31777	47._____

4 (#2)

48. 4312 Lowell La. Bloomfield Hills, MI	48301	4312 Lowell La. Bloomfield Hills, MI	48301	48._____
49. 6929 W. 135th Pl. Rapid City, SD	57709	6929 W. 135th Pl. Rapid City, SD	57509	49._____
50. 5143 Somerset Cir. Montauk, NY	11954	5143 Somerset Cir. Montauk, NY	11994	50._____
51. 8501 Kennedy St. West Chazy, NY	12992	8501 Kennedy St. West Chazy, NY	12992	51._____
52. 2164 E. McLean Ave. Hydro, OK	73048	2164 E. McLean Ave. Hydro, OK	73048	52._____
53. 7186 E St. NW Flint, MI	48501	7186 W St. NE Flint, MI	48051	53._____
54. 2121 Beechcrest Rd. Diamond, OH	44412	2121 Beachcrest Rd. Diamond, OH	44442	54._____
55. 3609 E. Montrose St. Valley Stream, NY	11581	3609 E. Montrose St. Valley Stream, NY	11581	55._____
56. 324 S. Alvadero St. San Antonio, TX	78207	324 S. Alvodero St. San Antonio, TX	78207	56._____
57. 2908 Gordon Rd. Albuquerque, NM	87101	2908 Gordon Rd. Albuquerque, NM	87011	57._____
58. 223 Great Falls Rd. Boston, MA	02101	233 Great Falls Rd. Boston, MA	02101	58._____
59. 201 Highwater Terr. Longs, SC	29568	201 Highwater Terr. Longs, SC	29658	59._____
60. 3201 Landover Rd. Charleston, WV	25328	3201 Landover Rd. Charleston, WV	25328	60._____

KEY (CORRECT ANSWERS)

1. A	11. A	21. D	31. D	41. B	51. A
2. C	12. A	22. D	32. A	42. A	52. A
3. C	13. C	23. A	33. B	43. C	53. D
4. A	14. A	24. A	34. C	44. C	54. D
5. B	15. A	25. A	35. D	45. D	55. A
6. A	16. B	26. B	36. D	46. A	56. B
7. D	17. D	27. A	37. C	47. B	57. C
8. C	18. A	28. C	38. A	48. A	58. B
9. D	19. A	29. C	39. A	49. C	59. C
10. C	20. C	30. A	40. A	50. C	60. A

TEST 3

DIRECTIONS: The following test contains 60 questions to be completed in 11 minutes. The two lists below—the correct list on the left and the list to be checked on the right—are to be compared quickly and accurately in that time. Mark your answer A, B, C or D based on the following information:

Mark "A" if the two items are exactly the same (no errors)
Mark "B" if there is an error in the address only
Mark "C" if there is an error in the ZIP code only
Mark "D" if there are errors in both the address and ZIP code
PRINT THE LETTER OF THE CORRECT ANSWER IN THE SPACE AT THE RIGHT.

	CORRECT LIST		LIST TO BE CHECKED		
1.	405 Winter Rd. NW Albany, GA	31706	405 Winter Rd. NW Albany, NY	37106	1._____
2.	607 S. Calaveras Rd. Starkville, MS	39759	607 S. Calaveras Rd. Starkville, MS	39759	2._____
3.	8406 La Casa St. Martin, KY	41649	8406 La Casa St. Martin, KY	41649	3._____
4.	121 N. Rippon St. Haiku, HI	96708	121 N. Rippen St. Haiku, HI	96708	4._____
5.	226 Stoerner Ave. Wideman, AR	72585	226 Stoerner Ave. Wideman, AK	72535	5._____
6.	3790 Serge St. Sodus, NY	14551	3790 Serge St. Sodus, NY	14551	6._____
7.	3429 Hermosa Dr. Huntingdon, PA	16652	3429 Hermosa Dr. Huntingdon, PA	15662	7._____
8.	3628 S. Zeeland St. Baltimore, MD	21205	3628 S. Zeeland St. Baltimore, MD	21025	8._____
9.	1330 Cheverly Ave. Belmar, NJ	07715	1330 Cheverley Ave. Belmar, NJ	07715	9._____
10.	1689 N. Derwood Dr. Arco, ID	83213	1689 N. Derwood Rd. Arco, ID	83213	10._____
11.	388 Sunrise Ct. Lawrence, KS	66049	388 Sunrise Ct. Lawrence, KS	66049	11._____
12.	635 Lehigh La. Orlando, FL	32862	653 Lehigh La. Orlando, FL	32362	12._____
13.	2560 Lansford Pl. Albion, PA	16401	2560 Landsford Pl. Albion, PA	16411	13._____

2 (#3)

#	Address 1	ZIP 1	Address 2	ZIP 2	Answer
14.	4631 Central Ave. Havre de Grace, MD	21078	4361 Central Ave. Havre de Grace, MD	21078	14.____
15.	24 Holiday Dr. Mason City, IA	50401	24 Holiday Dr. Mason City, IA	50701	15.____
16.	758 Los Arboles Ave. Bluffton, MN	56518	758 Los Arboles Ave. Bluffton, MN	56518	16.____
17.	3282 E. Downington St. Lynbrook, NY	11563	3282 E. Downington St. Lynbrook, NY	11563	17.____
18.	7117 Burlingham Ave. Tombstone, AZ	85638	7117 Burlingham Ave. Tombstone, AZ	85368	18.____
19.	32 Oaklawn Blvd. Syracuse, NY	13210	32 Oaklawn Blvd. Syracuse, NY	13210	19.____
20.	1274 Manzana Rd. Mesa, AZ	85207	1274 Manzona Rd. Mesa, AZ	80257	20.____
21.	4598 E. Kenilworth Dr. Logan, UT	84341	4598 E. Kenilworth Dr. Logan, UT	84341	21.____
22.	616 Berger Pl. Dayton, OK	73449	616 Berger Pl. Dayton, OK	73499	22.____
23.	1172 W. 83rd Ave. Louisville, KY	40298	1172 W. 83rd Ave. Louisville, KY	40298	23.____
24.	6434 E. Pulaski St. Atlantic City, NJ	08405	6434 E. Pulaski St. Atlantic City, NJ	08405	24.____
25.	2764 Rutherford Pl. Duluth, MN	55810	2674 Rutherford Pl. Duluth, MN	55810	25.____
26.	565 Greenville Blvd. Albany, NY	12222	565 Greenville Blvd. Albany, NY	12222	26.____
27.	319 Euclid Ave. Washington, DC	20013	391 Euclid Ave. Washington, DC	21003	27.____
28.	3824 Massasoit St. Honolulu, HI	96847	3824 Massasoit St. Honolulu, HI	96877	28.____
29.	22 Sagnaw Pkwy. Towson, MD	21286	22 Saginaw Pkwy. Towson, MD	21826	29.____
30.	2411 Chiofo Dr. Byram, CT	10573	2411 Chiofo Dr. Byram, CT	10753	30.____

31. 1928 S. Fairfield Ave. Ogden, AR	71853	1928 S. Farfield Ave. Ogden, AR	71853	31._____
32. 36218 Overhills Dr. Pensacola, FL	32597	36218 Overhills Dr. Pensacola, FL	32597	32._____
33. 5386 Fifth Ave. New York, NY	10025	5386 Fifth Ave. New York, NY	10025	33._____
34. 7526 Naraganset Pl. Paxico, KS	66526	7526 Naraganset Pl. Paxico, KS	65626	34._____
35. 52626 W. Oglesby Dr. Brooklyn, NY	11225	56226 W. Oglesby Dr. Brooklyn, NY	11235	35._____
36. 1003 Winchester Rd. Hershey, PA	17033	1003 Windchester Rd. Hershey, PA	17033	36._____
37. 347 Cavanaugh Ct. Covington, KY	41011	347 Cavanaugh Ct. Covington, KY	41011	37._____
38. 225 Robbins La. Kendall, CA	90551	225 Robbins La. Kendall, CA	90551	38._____
39. 225 El Camino Blvd. Sacramento, CA	95814	225 El Camino Blvd. Sacromento, CA	95844	39._____
40. 7310 Suncrest Dr. Wildwood, NJ	08260	7310 Suncrest Dr. Wildwood, NJ	08260	40._____
41. 1987 Wellington Ave. Roanoke, VA	24038	1897 Wellington Ave. Roanoke, VA	24088	41._____
42. 3124 S. 71st St. Altoona, PA	16601	3124 S. 71st St. Altoona, PA	16601	42._____
43. 729 Lincolnwood Blvd. Bloomington, IN	47401	729 Lincolnwood Blvd. Bloomington, IN	47401	43._____
44. 1166 N. Beaumont Dr. New Haven, CT	06533	1166 N. Beaumont Dr. New Maven, CT	06533	44._____
45. 3224 Winecona Pl. Norwalk, CT	06857	3224 Winecona Pl. Norwalk, CT	06357	45._____
46. 608 La Calle Bienvenida Madison, WI	53786	608 La Calle Bienvenida Madison, WI	53786	46._____
47. 808 Kinsella St. La Molte, IA	52045	808 Kinsella St. Le Molte, IA	52005	47._____

4 (#3)

48. 8625 Armitage Ave. NW Buffalo, NY	14203	8625 Arnitage Ave. NW Buffalo, NY	12403	48._____
49. 2343 Broadview Ave. Syosset, NY	11791	2343 Broadview Ave. Syosset, NY	17191	49._____
50. 4279 Grand Ave. Wakefield, RI	02880	4279 Grand Ave. Weakfield, RI	02880	50._____
51. 165 32nd Ave. Iowa City, IA	52246	165 32nd Ave. Iowa City, IA	52246	51._____
52. 12742 N. Deerborn St. Milwaukee, WI	53217	12742 N. Deerborn St. Milwaukee, WI	53217	52._____
53. 114 Estancia Ave. Daytona Beach, FL	32198	114 Estancia Ave. Daytona Beach, FL	32198	53._____
54. 351 S. Berwyn Rd. Riverhead, NY	11901	351 S. Berywn Rd. Riverhead, NY	11191	54._____
55. 7732 Hollywood Ave. Miami, FL	33126	7732 Hollywood Blvd. Miami, FL	33126	55._____
56. 6337 C St. SW Savannah, GA	31406	6637 C St. SW Savannah, GA	31406	56._____
57. 57895 E. Drexyl Ave. Akron, OH	44301	57895 E. Drexyl Ave. Akron, OH	44301	57._____
58. 19891 Overberry La. Altro, TX	75923	19891 Overberry La. Altro, TX	75523	58._____
59. 3465 S. Nashville St. Evansville, IN	47732	3465 S. Nashville St. Evansville, ID	43772	59._____
60. 1226 Odell Blvd. Bethlehem, PA	18015	1226 Odell Blvd. Bethleham, PA	18105	60._____

KEY (CORRECT ANSWERS)

1. D	11. A	21. A	31. B	41. D	51. A
2. A	12. D	22. C	32. A	42. A	52. A
3. A	13. D	23. A	33. A	43. A	53. A
4. B	14. B	24. A	34. C	44. B	54. D
5. D	15. C	25. B	35. D	45. C	55. B
6. A	16. A	26. A	36. B	46. A	56. B
7. C	17. A	27. D	37. A	47. D	57. A
8. C	18. C	28. C	38. A	48. D	58. C
9. B	19. A	29. D	39. D	49. C	59. D
10. B	20. D	30. C	40. A	50. B	60. D

TEST 4

DIRECTIONS: The following test contains 60 questions to be completed in 11 minutes. The two lists below—the correct list on the left and the list to be checked on the right—are to be compared quickly and accurately in that time. Mark your answer A, B, C or D based on the following information:
Mark "A" if the two items are exactly the same (no errors)
Mark "B" if there is an error in the address only
Mark "C" if there is an error in the ZIP code only
Mark "D" if there are errors in both the address and ZIP code
PRINT THE LETTER OF THE CORRECT ANSWER IN THE SPACE AT THE RIGHT.

	CORRECT LIST		LIST TO BE CHECKED		
1.	94002 Chappel Ct. Stamford, CT	06926	94002 Chappel Ct. Stamford, CT	06926	1._____
2.	512 La Vega Dr. Myrtle Beach, SC	29575	512 La Vega Dr. Myrtle Beach, SC	29575	2._____
3.	8774 W. Winona Pl. Columbia, SC	29201	8774 W. Winona Pl. Columbia, SC	29021	3._____
4.	6431 Ingleside St. Virginia Beach, VA	23450	6431 Ingleside St. Virginia Beach, VA	24350	4._____
5.	227 N. Leanington St. Providence, RI	02909	227 N. Leenington St. Providence, RI	02909	5._____
6.	2355 Estrada Blvd. New York, NY	11225	2335 Estrada Blvd. New York, NY	12225	6._____
7.	3987 E. Westwood Ave. Green Bay, WI	54304	3987 W. Eastwood Ave. Green Bay, WI	54034	7._____
8.	117 Appleseed Ct. Skamokawa, WA	98647	117 Appleseed Ct. Skamokawa, WA	99647	8._____
9.	2674 E. Champlain Cir. Quogue, NY	11959	2674 E. Champlain Cir. Quogue, NY	11959	9._____
10.	8751 Elmhurst Blvd. Ames, IA	50014	8751 Elmhurst Blvd. Amos, IA	50014	10._____
11.	664 Solano Dr. Erie, PA	16541	664 Solaro Dr. Erie, PA	16541	11._____
12.	4423 S. Escenaba St. Woonsocket, RI	02895	4423 S. Escanaba St. Woonsocket, RI	02895	12._____
13.	1198 N St. NW Canton, OH	44798	1198 N St. NW Canton, OH	44798	13._____

14. 4004 Kolb Ct. Sparta, GA	31087	4004 Kolb Ct. Sparta, GA	31087	14._____
15. 96753 Wrightwood Ave. Pawleys Island, SC	29585	96753 Wrightwood Ave. Pauleys Island, SC	25985	15._____
16. 2445 Sangamow Ave. North Valley Stream, NY	11580	2445 Sangamow Ave. North Valley Stream, NY	11580	16._____
17. 5117 E. 67th Pl. Seattle, WA	98198	5117 E. 67th St. Seattle, WA	99198	17._____
18. 847 Mesa Grande Pl. Ocala, FL	34477	847 Mesa Grande Pl. Ocala, FL	37744	18._____
19. 1100 Cermaken St. Waterford, CT	06385	1100 Cermaken St. Waterfort, CT	06685	19._____
20. 321 Tijeras Ave. NW Atlanta, GA	30301	321 Tijeras Ave. NW Atlanta, GA	30301	20._____
21. 3405 Prospect St. Olympia, WA	98501	3045 Prospect St. Olympia, WA	89501	21._____
22. 6643 Burlington Pl. Adams, TN	37010	6643 Burlington Pl. Adams, TN	37010	22._____
23. 851 Esperanza Blvd. Tully, NY	13159	851 Esparanza Blvd. Tully, NY	13199	23._____
24. 212 Marshall St. Jenkinjones, WV	24848	212 Marshall St. Jenkinjones, WV	24848	24._____
25. 1008 Pennsylvania Ave. Washington, DC	20002	1008 Pennsylvania Ave. Washington, DC	20008	25._____
26. 2924 26th St. N Great Falls, MT	59401	2924 26th St. N Great Falls, MT	59041	26._____
27. 7115 Highland Dr. Chattanooga, TN	37404	7115 Highland Dr. Chatanooga, TN	37404	27._____
28. 379 Francis Pkwy. Chaptico, MD	20621	379 Francis Pkwy. Chaptico, MA	20621	28._____
29. 3508 Camron Mills Rd. Gibson, PA	18820	3508 Camron Mills Rd. Gibson, PA	18820	29._____
30. 67158 Capston Dr. Morgantown, WV	26505	67158 Capston Dr. Morgantown, WV	26055	30._____

31. 3613 S. Taylor Ave. Acton, MT	59002	3613 S. Taylor Ave. Action, MT	58002	31._____
32. 2421 Menokin Dr. Coyote, NM	87012	2421 Menokin Dr. Coyote, NM	87012	32._____
33. 3226 M St. NW Durham, NC	27717	3226 N St. NW Durham, NC	27717	33._____
34. 1201 Court House Rd. Santa Fe, NM	87500	1201 Court House Rd. Santa Fe, NM	87500	34._____
35. 75 Caswell Pl. Findlay, OH	45840	75 Caswell Pl. Findley, OH	45340	35._____
36. 17 Bennett St. Media, PA	19091	17 Bennet St. Media, PA	19901	36._____
37. 7 Vine Bowl Dr. Adams, NE	68301	7 Wine Bowl Dr. Adams, NE	68801	37._____
38. 126 McKinley Ave. Raleigh, NC	27603	126 McKinley Ave. Raleigh, NC	27608	38._____
39. 384 Nepperhan Rd. Rochester, NY	14622	384 Nepperhan Rd. Rochester, NY	14622	39._____
40. 1077 Contreras Ave. Chicago, IL	60615	1077 Contreras Ave. Chicago, IL	60615	40._____
41. 111 Caroline Pl. Jackson, TN	38301	111 Caroline Pl. Jackson, TN	38001	41._____
42. 21 Greenleaf Blvd. Rye, NY	10580	21 Greenleaf Blvd. Rye, NJ	10580	42._____
43. 245 Rumsey Rd. Yonkers, NY	10705	245 Ramsey Rd. Yonkers, NY	10705	43._____
44. 927 South St. Peekskill, NY	10566	927 South St. Peekskill, NY	10656	44._____
45. 44 Monroe Ave. Larchmont, NY	10538	44 Monroe Ave. Larchmont, NY	10538	45._____
46. 39 Andrea La. Scarsdale, NY	10583	39 Andrea La. Scarsdale, NY	10588	46._____
47. 1006 Baumgartner Rd. Ruland, WY	62143	1006 Baumgardner Rd. Ruland, WY	62443	47._____

48. 51 Cypress Rd. New Hope, PA	18938	51 Cypress Rd. New Hape, PA	19938	48._____
49. 213 Shore Lane Rd. Elkton, MD	21922	213 Shore Lane Rd. Elkton, MD	21192	49._____
50. 189 Columbus Ave. Silver Spring, MD	20916	189 Columbus Ave. Silver Spring, MD	20916	50._____
51. 124 W. Stationery Rd. Beckley, WV	25801	124 W. Stationery Rd. Beckley, WV	25801	51._____
52. 650 Pinecrest Ct. Purdy, VT	03124	650 Pinecrest Ct. Purdy, VT	03124	52._____
53. 129 Tewksbury Rd. Mackinaw, IL	61755	129 Tewksbury Rd. Mackinaw, IN	61175	53._____
54. 100 Gallow Hill Rd. SW San Antonio, TX	78298	100 Gallow Hill Rd. SE San Antonio, TX	78288	54._____
55. 234 Myrtle Ave. Greensboro, NC	27499	234 Myrtle Ave. Greenboro, NC	27499	55._____
56. 35 Chase Pl. NE Cook, NE	68329	35 Chase Pl. NE Cooke, NC	68239	56._____
57. 14 Terrace Ave. Tyler, TX	75798	14 Terrace Ave. Tyler, TX	75798	57._____
58. 35 Collins Point Rd. Zephyr, TX	76890	35 Collins Point Rd. Zephyr, TX	76890	58._____
59. 164 Sagmor Ct. Omaha, NE	68197	164 Sagmor St. Omaha, NE	68797	59._____
60. 117 Warburton Dr. Oak Park, IL	60301	117 Warbarton Dr. Oak Park, IL	60801	60._____

KEY (CORRECT ANSWERS)

1. A	11. B	21. D	31. D	41. C	51. A
2. A	12. B	22. A	32. A	42. B	52. A
3. C	13. A	23. D	33. B	43. B	53. D
4. C	14. A	24. A	34. A	44. C	54. D
5. B	15. D	25. C	35. D	45. A	55. B
6. D	16. A	26. C	36. D	46. C	56. D
7. D	17. D	27. B	37. D	47. D	57. A
8. C	18. C	28. B	38. C	48. D	58. A
9. A	19. D	29. A	39. A	49. C	59. D
10. B	20. A	30. C	40. A	50. A	60. D

NAME AND NUMBER CHECKING
EXAMINATION SECTION
TEST 1

DIRECTIONS: Questions 1 through 17 consist of sets of names and addresses. In each question, the name and address in Column II should be an exact copy of the name and address in Column I.
If there is:
a mistake only in the name, mark your answer A;
a mistake only in the address, mark your answer B;
a mistake in both name and address, mark your answer C;
No mistake in either name or address, mark your answer D.

Sample Question

Column I
Christina Magnusson
288 Greene Street
New York, N.Y. 10003

Column II
Christina Magnusson
288 Greene Street
New York, N.Y. 10013

Since there is a mistake only in the address (the zip code should be 10003 instead of 10013), the answer to the sample question is B.

COLUMN I | COLUMN II

1. Ms. Joan Kelly
313 Franklin Avenue
Brooklyn, N.Y. 11202

Ms. Joan Kielly
318 Franklin Ave.
Brooklyn, N.Y. 11202

1.____

2. Mrs. Eileen Engel
47-24 86 Road
Queens, N.Y. 11122

Mrs. Ellen Engel
47-24 86 Road
Queens, New York 11122

2.____

3. Marcia Michaels
213 E. 81 St.
New York, N.Y. 10012

Marcia Michaels
213 E. 81 St.
New York, N.Y. 10012

3.____

4. Rev. Edward J. Smyth
1401 Brandeis Street
San Francisco, Calif. 96201

Rev. Edward J. Smyth
1401 Brandies Street
San Francisco, Calif. 96201

4.____

5. Alicia Rodriguez
24-68 82 St.
Elmhurst, N.Y. 11122

Alicia Rodriguez
2468 81 St.
Elmhurst, N.Y. 11122

5.____

COLUMN I	COLUMN II	
6. Ernest Eisemann 21 Columbia St. New York, N.Y. 10007	Ernest Eisermann 21 Columbia St. New York, N.Y. 10007	6.____
7. Mr. & Mrs. George Petersson 87-11 91st Avenue Woodhaven, N.Y. 11421	Mr. & Mrs. George Peterson 87-11 91st Avenue Woodhaven, N.Y. 11421	7.____
8. Mr. Ivan Klebnikov 1848 Newkirk Avenue Brooklyn, N.Y. 11226	Mr. Ivan Klebikov 1848 Newkirk Avenue Brooklyn, N.Y. 11622	8.____
9. Mr. Samuel Rothfleisch 71 Pine Street New York, N.Y. 10005	Samuel Rothfleisch 71 Pine Street New York, N.Y. 100005	9.____
10. Mrs. Isabel Tonnessen 198 East 185th Street Bronx, N.Y. 10458	Mrs. Isabel Tonnessen 189 East 185th Street Bronx, N.Y. 10348	10.____
11. Esteban Perez 173 Eighth Street Staten Island, N.Y. 10306	Estaban Perez 173 Eighth Street Staten Island, N.Y. 10306	11.____
12. Esta Wong 141 West 68 St. New York, N.Y. 10023	Esta Wang 141 West 68 St. New York, N.Y. 10023	12.____
13. Dr. Alberto Grosso 3475 12th Avenue Brooklyn, N.Y. 11218	Dr. Alberto Grosso 3475 12th Avenue Brooklyn, N.Y. 11218	13.____
14. Mrs. Ruth Bortias 482 Theresa Ct. Far Rockaway, N.Y. 11691	Ms. Ruth Bortlas 482 Theresa Ct. Far Rockaway, N.Y. 11169	14.____
15. Mr. & Mrs. Howard Fox 2301 Sedgwick Ave. Bronx, N.Y. 10468	Mr. & Mrs. Howard Fox 231 Sedgwick Ave. Bronx, N.Y. 10468	15.____
16. Miss Marjorie Black 223 East 23 Street New York, N.Y. 10010	Miss Margorie Black 223 East 23 Street New York, N.Y. 10010	16.____

COLUMN I	COLUMN II	
17. Michelle Herman 806 Valley Rd. Old Tappan, N.J. 07675	Michelle Hermann 806 Valley Dr. Old Tappan, N.J. 07675	17.____

KEY (CORRECT ANSWERS)

1.	C	7.	A	13.	D
2.	A	8.	C	14.	C
3.	D	9.	D	15.	B
4.	B	10.	B	16.	A
5.	B	11.	A	17.	C
6.	A	12.	D		

TEST 2

DIRECTIONS: Questions 1 through 15 are to be answered SOLELY on the instructions given below. *PRINT THE LETTER OF THE CORRECT ANSWER IN THE SPACE AT THE RIGHT.*

INSTRUCTIONS

In each of the following questions, the 3-line name and address in Column I is the masterlist entry, and the 3-line entry in Column II is the information to be checked against the master list. If there is one line that does not match, mark your answer A; if there are two lines that do not match, mark your answer B; if all three lines do not match, mark your answer C; if the lines all match exactly, mark your answer D.

Sample Question

Column I	Column II
Mark L. Field	Mark L. Field
11-09 Price Park Blvd.	11-99 Prince Park Way
Bronx, N.Y. 11402	Bronx, N.Y. 11401

The first lines in each column match exactly. The second lines do not match since 11-09 does not match 11-<u>99</u>; and Blvd. does not match <u>Way</u>. The third lines do not match either since 1140<u>2</u> does not match 1140<u>1</u>. Therefore, there are two lines that do not match, and the CORRECT answer is B.

COLUMN I | COLUMN II

1. Jerome A. Jackson
   1243 14th Avenue
   New York, N.Y. 10023

   Jerome A. Johnson
   1234 14th Avenue
   New York, N.Y. 10023

   1.____

2. Sophie Strachtheim
   33-28 Connecticut Ave.
   Far Rockaway, N.Y. 11697

   Sophie Strachtheim
   33-28 Connecticut Ave.
   Far Rockaway, N.Y. 11697

   2.____

3. Elisabeth N.T. Gorrell
   256 Exchange St.
   New York, N.Y. 10013

   Elizabeth N.T. Gorrell
   256 Exchange St.
   New York, N.Y. 10013

   3.____

4. Maria J. Gonzalez
   7516 E. Sheepshead Rd.
   Brooklyn, N.Y. 11240

   Maria J. Gonzalez
   7516 N. Shepshead Rd.
   Brooklyn, N.Y. 11240

   4.____

5. Leslie B. Brautenweiler
   21 57A Seiler Terr.
   Flushing, N.Y. 11367

   Leslie B. Brautenwieler
   21-75A Seiler Terr.
   Flushing, N.J. 11367

   5.____

COLUMN I	COLUMN II	
6. Rigoberto J. Peredes 157 Twin Towers, #18F Tottenville, S. I., N.Y,	Rigoberto J. Peredes 157 Twin Towers, #18F Tottenville, S.I., N.Y.	6.____
7. Pietro F. Albino P.O. Box 7548 Floral Park, N.Y. 11005	Pietro F. Albina P.O. Box 7458 Floral Park, N.Y. 11005	7.____
8. Joanne Zimmerman Bldg. SW, Room 314 532-4601	Joanne Zimmermann Bldg. SW, Room 314 532-4601	8.____
9. Carlyle Whetstone Payroll Div. –A, Room 212A 262-5000, ext. 471	Carlyle Whetstone Payroll Div. –A, Room 212A 262-5000, ext. 417	9.____
10. Kenneth Chiang Legal Council, Room 9745 (201) 416-9100, ext. 17	Kenneth Chiang Legal Counsel, Room 9745 (201) 416-9100, Ext. 17	10.____
11. Ethel Koenig Personnel Services Division, Room 433; 635-7572	Ethel Hoenig Personal Services Division, Room 433; 635-7527	11.____
12. Joyce Ehrhardt Office of the Administrator, Room W56; 387-8706	Joyce Ehrhart Office of the Administrator, Room W56; 387-7806	12.____
13. Ruth Lang EAM Bldg., Room C101 625-2000, ext. 765	Ruth Lang EAM Bldg., Room C110 625-2000, ext. 765	13.____
14. Anne Marie Ionozzi Investigations, Room 827 576-4000, ext. 832	Anna Marie Ionozzi Investigation, Room 827 566-4000, ext. 832	14.____
15. Willard Jameson Fm C Bldg., Room 687 454-3010	Willard Jamieson Fm C Bldg., Room 687 454-3010	15.____

KEY (CORRECT ANSWERS)

1. B 6. D   11. C
2. D 7. B   12. B
3. A 8. D   13. A
4. A 9. B   14. C
5. C 10. A 15. A

TEST 3

DIRECTIONS: Questions 1 through 10 are to be answered on the basis of the following instructions. *PRINT THE LETTER OF THE CORRECT ANSWER IN THE SPACE AT THE RIGHT.*

INSTRUCTIONS

For each such set of names, addresses, and numbers listed in Columns I and II, select your answer from the following options:
The names in Columns I and II are different,
The addresses in Columns I and II are different,
The numbers in Columns I and II are different,
The names, addresses, and numbers in Columns I and II are identical.

	COLUMN I	COLUMN II	
1.	Francis Jones 62 Stately Avenue 96-12446	Francis Jones 62 Stately Avenue 96-21446	1.____
2.	Julio Montez 19 Ponderosa Road 56-73161	Julio Montez 19 Ponderosa Road 56-71361	2.____
3.	Mary Mitchell 2314 Melbourne Drive 68-92172	Mary Mitchell 2314 Melbourne Drive 68-92172	3.____
4.	Harry Patterson 25 Dunne Street 14-33430	Harry Patterson 25 Dunne Street 14-34330	4.____
5.	Patrick Murphy 171 West Hosmer Street 93-81214	Patrick Murphy 171 West Hosmer Street 93-18214	5.____
6.	August Schultz 816 St. Clair Avenue 53-40149	August Schultz 816 St. Claire Avenue 53-40149	6.____
7.	George Taft 72 Runnymede Street 47-04033	George Taft 72 Runnymede Street 47-04023	7.____
8.	Angus Henderson 1418 Madison Street 81-76375	Angus Henderson 1318 Madison Street 81-76375	8.____

COLUMN I   COLUMN II

9. Carolyn Mazur   Carolyn Mazur   9._____
    12 Riverview Road   12 Rivervane Road
    38-99615   38-99615

10. Adele Russell   Adela Russell   10._____
    1725 Lansing Lane   1725 Lansing Lane
    72-91962   72-91962

KEY (CORRECT ANSWERS)

1.	C	6.	B
2.	C	7.	C
3.	D	8.	D
4.	C	9.	B
5.	C	10.	A

TEST 4

DIRECTIONS: Questions 1 through 20 test how good you are at catching mistakes in typing or printing. In each question, the name and address in Column II should be an exact copy of the name and address in Column I. Mark your answer
  A. If there is no mistake in either name or address;
  B. If there is a mistake in both name and address;
  C. If there is a mistake only in the name;
  D. If there is a mistake only in the address.
PRINT THE LETTER OF THE CORRECT ANSWER IN THE SPACE AT THE RIGHT.

<u>COLUMN I</u>   <u>COLUMN II</u>

1. Milos Yanocek
   33-60 14 Street
   Long Island City, N.Y. 11011

   Milos Yanocek
   33-60 14 Street
   Long Island City, N.Y. 11001

   1.____

2. Alphonse Sabattelo
   24 Minnetta Lane
   New York, N.Y. 10006

   Alphonse Sabbattelo
   24 Minetta Lane
   New York, N.Y. 10006

   2.____

3. Helen Steam
   5 Metropolitan Oval
   Bronx, N.Y. 10462

   Helene Stearn
   5 Metropolitan Oval
   Bronx, N.Y. 10462

   3.____

4. Jacob Weisman
   231 Francis Lewis Boulevard
   Forest Hills, N.Y. 11325

   Jacob Weisman
   231 Francis Lewis Boulevard
   Forest Hills, N.Y. 11325

   4.____

5. Riccardo Fuente
   134 West 83 Street
   New York, N.Y. 10024

   Riccardo Fuentes
   134 West 88 Street
   New York, N.Y. 10024

   5.____

6. Dennis Lauber
   52 Avenue D
   Brooklyn, N.Y. 11216

   Dennis Lauder
   52 Avenue D
   Brooklyn, N.Y. 11216

   6.____

7. Paul Cutter
   195 Galloway Avenue
   Staten Island, N.Y. 10356

   Paul Cutter
   175 Galloway Avenue
   Staten Island, N.Y. 10365

   7.____

8. Sean Donnelly
   45-58 41 Avenue
   Woodside, N.Y. 11168

   Sean Donnelly
   45-58 41 Avenue
   Woodside, N.Y. 11168

   8.____

9. Clyde Willot
   1483 Rockaway Avenue
   Brooklyn, N.Y. 11238

   Clyde Willat
   1483 Rockaway Avenue
   Brooklyn, N.Y. 11238

   9.____

COLUMN I	COLUMN II	
10. Michael Stanakis 419 Sheriden Avenue Staten Island, N.Y. 10363	Michael Stanakis 419 Sheraden Avenue Staten Island, N.Y. 10363	10.____
11. Joseph DiSilva 63-84 Saunders Road Rego Park, N.Y. 11431	Joseph Disilva 64-83 Saunders Road Rego Park, N.Y. 11431	11.____
12. Linda Polansky 2224 Fendon Avenue Bronx, N.Y. 20464	Linda Polansky 2255 Fenton Avenue Bronx, N.Y. 10464	12.____
13. Alfred Klein 260 Hillside Terrace Staten Island, N.Y. 15545	Alfred Klein 260 Hillside Terrace Staten Island, N.Y. 15545	13.____
14. William McDonnell 504 E. 55 Street New York, N.Y. 10103	William McConnell 504 E. 55 Street New York, N.Y. 10108	14.____
15. Angela Cipolla 41-11 Parson Avenue Flushing, N.Y. 11446	Angela Cipola 41-11 Parsons Avenue Flushing, N.Y. 11446	15.____
16. Julie Sheridan 1212 Ocean Avenue Brooklyn, N.Y. 11237	Julia Sheridan 1212 Ocean Avenue Brooklyn, N.Y. 11237	16.____
17. Arturo Rodriguez 2156 Cruger Avenue Bronx, N.Y. 10446	Arturo Rodrigues 2156 Cruger Avenue Bronx, N.Y. 10446	17.____
18. Helen McCabe 2044 East 19 Street Brooklyn, N.Y. 11204	Helen McCabe 2040 East 19 Street Brooklyn, N.Y. 11204	18.____
19. Charles Martin 526 West 160 Street New York, N.Y. 10022	Charles Martin 526 West 160 Street New York, N.Y. 10022	19.____
20. Morris Rabinowitz 31 Avenue M Brooklyn, N.Y. 11216	Morris Rabinowitz 31 Avenue N Brooklyn, N.Y. 11216	20.____

KEY (CORRECT ANSWERS)

1.	D	11.	B
2.	B	12.	D
3.	C	13.	A
4.	A	14.	B
5.	B	15.	B
6.	C	16.	C
7.	D	17.	C
8.	A	18.	D
9.	B	19.	A
10.	D	20.	D

TEST 5

DIRECTIONS: In copying the addresses below from Column A to the same line in Column B, an Agent-in-Training made some errors. For Questions 1 through 5, if you find that the agent made an error in
only one line, mark your answer A;
only two lines, mark your answer B;
only three lines, mark your answer C;
all four lines, mark your answer D.

EXAMPLE

COLUMN A	COLUMN B
24 Third Avenue	24 Third Avenue
5 Lincoln Road	5 Lincoln Street
50 Central Park West	6 Central Park West
37-21 Queens Boulevard	21-37 Queens Boulevard

Since errors were made on only three lines, namely the second, third, and fourth, the CORRECT answer is C.
PRINT THE LETTER OF THE CORRECT ANSWER IN THE SPACE AT THE RIGHT.

COLUMN A   COLUMN B

1. 57-22 Springfield Boulevard   75-22 Springfield Boulevard   1.____
    94 Gun Hill Road   94 Gun Hill Avenue
    8 New Dorp Lane   8 New Drop Lane
    36 Bedford Avenue   36 Bedford Avenue

2. 538 Castle Hill Avenue   538 Castle Hill Avenue   2.____
    54-15 Beach Channel Drive   54-15 Beach Channel Drive
    21 Ralph Avenue   21 Ralph Avenue
    162 Madison Avenue   162 Morrison Avenue

3. 49 Thomas Street   49 Thomas Street   3.____
    27-21 Northern Blvd.   21-27 Northern Blvd.
    86 125th Street   86 125th Street
    872 Atlantic Ave.   872 Baltic Ave,

4. 261-17 Horace Harding Expwy.   261-17 Horace Harding Pkwy.   4.____
    191 Fordham Road   191 Fordham Road
    6 Victory Blvd.   6 Victoria Blvd.
    552 Oceanic Ave.   552 Ocean Ave.

5. 90-05 38th Avenue   90-05 36th Avenue   5.____
    19 Central Park West   19 Central Park East
    9281 Avenue X   9281 Avenue X
    22 West Farms Square   22 West Farms Square

KEY (CORRECT ANSWERS)

1. C
2. A
3. B
4. C
5. B

TEST 6

DIRECTIONS: For Questions 1 through 10, choose the letter in Column II next to the number which EXACTLY matches the number in Column I. *PRINT THE LETTER OF THE CORRECT ANSWER IN THE SPACE AT THE RIGHT.*

	COLUMN I	COLUMN II	
1.	14235	A. 13254 B. 12435 C. 13245 D. 14235	1.____
2.	70698	A. 90768 B. 60978 C. 70698] D. 70968	2.____
3.	11698	A. 11689 B. 11986 C. 11968 D. 11698	3.____
4.	50497	A. 50947 B. 50497 C. 50749 D. 54097	4.____
5.	69635	A. 60653 B. 69630 C. 69365 D. 69635	5.____
6.	1201022011	A. 1201022011 B. 1201020211 C. 1202012011 D. 1021202011	6.____
7.	3893981389	A. 3893891389 B. 3983981389 C. 3983891389 D. 3893981389	7.____
8.	4765476589	A. 4765476598 B. 4765476588 C. 4765476589 D. 4765746589	8.____

9. 8679678938
   A. 8679687938
   B. 8679678938
   C. 8697678938
   D. 8678678938

9._____

10. 6834836932
   A. 6834386932
   B. 6834836923
   C. 6843836932
   D. 6834836932

10._____

Questions 11-15.

DIRECTIONS: For Questions 11 through 15, determine how many of the symbols in Column Z are exactly the same as the symbol in Column Y.
If none is exactly the same, answer A;
If only one symbol is exactly the same, answer B;
If two symbols are exactly the same, answer C;
If three symbols are exactly the same, answer D.

COLUMN Y | COLUMN Z

11. A123B1266

A123B1366
A123B1266
A133B1366
A123B1266

11._____

12. CC28D3377

CD22D3377
CC38D3377
CC28C3377
CC28D2277

12._____

13. M21AB201X

M12AB201X
M21AB201X
M21AB201Y
M21BA201X

13._____

14. PA383Y744

AP383Y744
PA338Y744
PA388Y744
PA383Y774

14._____

15. PB2Y8893

PB2Y8893
PB2Y8893
PB3Y8898
PB2Y8893

15._____

KEY (CORRECT ANSWERS)

1.	D	6.	A	11.	C
2.	C	7.	D	12.	A
3.	D	8.	C	13.	B
4.	B	9.	B	14.	A
5.	D	10.	D	15.	D

NAME AND NUMBER CHECKING
EXAMINATION SECTION
TEST 1

DIRECTIONS: Each question or incomplete statement is followed by several suggested answers or completions. Select the one that BEST answers the question or completes the statement. *PRINT THE LETTER OF THE CORRECT ANSWER IN THE SPACE AT THE RIGHT.*

Questions 1-10.

DIRECTIONS: Questions 1 through 10 below present the identification numbers, initials, and last names of employees enrolled in a city retirement system. You are to choose the option (A, B, C, or D) that has the identical identification number, initials, and last name as those given in each question.

SAMPLE QUESTION

B145695 JL Jones
    A. B146798 JL Jones   B. B145698 JL Jonas
    C. P145698 JL Jones   C. B145698 JL Jones

The correct answer is D. Only option D shows the identification number, initials, and last name exactly as they are in the sample question. Options A, B, and C have errors in the identification number or last name.

1. J297483 PL Robinson
   A. J294783 PL Robinson   B. J297483 PL Robinson
   C. K297483 PL Robinson   D. J297843 PL Robinson

1._____

2. S497662 JG Schwartz
   A. S497662 JG Schwarz   B. S497762 JG Schwartz
   C. S497662 JG Schwartz   D. S497663 JG Schwartz

2._____

3. G696436 LN Alberton
   A. G696436 LM Alberton   B. G696436 LN Albertson
   C. G696346 LN Albertson   D. G696436 LN Alberton

3._____

4. R774923 AD Aldrich
   A. R774923 AD Aldrich   B. R744923 AD Aldrich
   C. R774932 AP Aldrich   D. R774932 AD Allrich

4._____

5. N239638 RP Hrynyk
   A. N236938 PR Hrynyk   B. N236938 RP Hrynyk
   C. N239638 PR Hrynyk   D. N239638 RP Hrynyk

5._____

6. R156949 LT Carlson
   A. R156949 LT Carlton
   B. R156494 LT Carlson
   C. R159649 LT Carlton
   D. R156949 LT Carlson

   6._____

7. T524697 MN Orenstein
   A. T524697 MN Orenstein
   B. T524967 MN Orinstein
   C. T524697 NM Ornstein
   D. T524967 NM Orenstein

   7._____

8. L346239 JD Remsen
   A. L346239 JD Remson
   B. L364239 JD Remsen
   C. L346438 JD Remsen
   D. L346239 JD Remsen

   8._____

9. P966438 SB Rieperson
   A. P966438 SB Reiperson
   B. P966438 SB Reiperson
   C. R996438 SB Rieperson
   D. P966438 SB Rieperson

   9._____

10. D749382 CD Thompson
    A. P749382 CD Thompson
    B. D749832 CD Thomsonn
    C. D749382 CD Thompson
    D. D749823 CD Thomspon

    10._____

Questions 11-20.

DIRECTIONS: Each of Questions 11 through 20 gives the identification number and name of a person who has received treatment at a certain hospital. You are to choose the option (A, B, C, or D) which has EXACTLY the same identification number and name as those given in the question.

SAMPLE QUESTION

123765 Frank Y. Jones
   A. 123675 Frank Y. Jones
   B. 123765 Frank T. Jones
   C. 123765 Frank Y. Johns
   D. 123765 Frank Y. Jones

The correct answer is D. Only option D shows the identification number and name exactly as they are in the sample question. Option A has a mistake in the identification number. Option B has a mistake in the middle initial of the name. Option C has a mistake in the last name.

Now answer Questions 11 through 20 in the same manner.

11. 754898 Diane Malloy
    A. 745898 Diane Malloy
    B. 754898 Dion Malloy
    C. 754898 Diane Malloy
    D. 754898 Diane Maloy

    11._____

12. 661818 Ferdinand Figueroa
    A. 661818 Ferdinand Figeuroa
    B. 661618 Ferdinand Figueroa
    C. 661818 Ferdnand Figueroa
    D. 661818 Ferdinand Figueroa

    12._____

13. 100101 Norman D. Braustein 13.____
    A. 100101 Norman D. Braustein   B. 101001 Norman D. Braustein
    C. 100101 Norman P. Braustien   D. 100101 Norman D. Bruastein

14. 838696 Robert Kittredge 14.____
    A. 838969 Robert Kittredge   B. 838696 Robert Kittredge
    C. 388696 Robert Kittredge   D. 838696 Robert Kittridge

15. 243716 Abraham Soletsky 15.____
    A. 243716 Abrahm Soletsky   B. 243716 Abraham Solestky
    C. 243176 Abraham Soletsky   D. 243716 Abraham Soletsky

16. 981121 Phillip M. Maas 16.____
    A. 981121 Phillip M. Mass   B. 981211 Phillip M. Maas
    C. 981121 Phillip M. Maas   D. 981121 Phillip N. Maas

17. 786556 George Macalusso 17.____
    A. 785656 George Macalusso   B. 786556 George Macalusso
    C. 786556 George Maculasso   D. 786556 George Macluasso

18. 639472 Eugene Weber 18.____
    A. 639472 Eugene Weber   B. 639472 Eugene Webre
    C. 693472 Eugene Weber   D. 639742 Eugene Weber

19. 724936 John J. Lomonaco 19.____
    A. 724936 John J. Lomanoco   B. 724396 John J. Lomonaco
    C. 724936 John J. Lomonaco   D. 724936 John J. Lamonaco

20. 899868 Michael Schnitzer 20.____
    A. 899868 Micheal Schnitzer   B. 898968 Michael Schnizter
    C. 899688 Michael Schnitzer   D. 899868 Michael Schnitzer

Questions 21-28.

DIRECTIONS: Questions 21 through 28 consist of lines of names, dates, and numbers which represent the names, membership dates, social security numbers, and members of the retirement system. For each question you are to choose the option (A, B, C, or D) which exactly matches the information in the question.

SAMPLE QUESTION

Crossen 12/23/56 173568929 25349
  A. Crossen 2/23/56 173568929 253492
  B. Crossen 12/23/56 173568719 253492
  C. Crossen 12/23/56 173568929 253492
  D. Crossan 12/23/56 173568929 258492

The correct answer is C. Only option C shows the name, date, and numbers exactly as they are in Column I. Option A has a mistake in the date. Option B has a mistake in the social security number. Option D has a mistake in the name and in the membership number.

21. Figueroa 1/15/64 119295386 21.____
    A. Figueroa 1/5/64 119295386 147563
    B. Figueroa 1/15/64 119295386 147563
    C. Figueroa 1/15/64 119295836 147563
    D. Figueroa 1/15/64 119295886 147563

22. Goodridge 6/19/59 106237869 128352 22.____
    A. Goodridge 6/19/59 106287869 128332
    B. Goodrigde 6/19/59 106237869 128352
    C. Goodridge 6/9/59 106237869 128352
    D. Goodridge 6/19/59 106237869 128352

23. Balsam 9/13/57 109652382 116938 23.____
    A. Balsan 9/13/57 109652382 116938
    B. Balsam 9/13/57 109652382 116938
    C. Balsom 9/13/57 109652382 116938
    D. Balsalm 9/13/57 109652382 116938

24. Mackenzie 2/16/49 127362513 101917 24.____
    A. Makenzie 2/16/49 127362513 101917
    B. Mackenzie 2/16/49 127362513 101917
    C. Mackenzie 2/16/49 127362513 101977
    D. Mackenzie 2/16/49 127862513 101917

25. Halpern 12/2/73 115205359 286070 25.____
    A. Halpern 12/2/73 115206359 286070
    B. Halpern 12/2/73 113206359 286070
    C. Halpern 12/2/73 115206359 206870
    D. Halpern 12/2/73 115206359 286870

26. Phillips 4/8/66 137125516 192612 26.____
    A. Phillips 4/8/66 137125516 196212
    B. Philipps 4/8/66 137125516 192612
    C. Phillips 4/8/66 137125516 192612
    D. Phillips 4/8/66 137122516 192612

27. Francisce 11/9/63 123926037 152210 27.____
    A. Francisce 11/9/63 123826837 152210
    B. Francisce 11/9/63 123926037 152210
    C. Francisce 11/9/63 123936037 152210
    D. Franscice 11/9/63 123926037 152210

28. Silbert 7/28/54 118421999 178514   28.____
     A. Silbert 7/28/54 118421999 178544
     B. Silbert 7/28/54 184421999 178514
     C. Silbert 7/28/54 118421999 178514
     D. Siblert 7/28/54 118421999 178514

KEY (CORRECT ANSWERS)

1.	B	11.	C	21.	B
2.	C	12.	D	22.	D
3.	D	13.	A	23.	B
4.	A	14.	B	24.	B
5.	D	15.	D	25.	A
6.	D	16.	C	26.	C
7.	A	17.	B	27.	B
8.	D	18.	A	28.	C
9.	D	19.	C		
10.	C	20.	D		

TEST 2

DIRECTIONS: Each question or incomplete statement is followed by several suggested answers or completions. Select the one that BEST answers the question or completes the statement. *PRINT THE LETTER OF THE CORRECT ANSWER IN THE SPACE AT THE RIGHT.*

Questions 1-3.

DIRECTIONS: Items 1 through 3 are a test of your proofreading ability. Each item consists of Copy I and Copy II. You are to assume that Copy I in each item is correct. Copy II, which is meant to be a duplicate of Copy I, may contain some typographical errors. In each item, compare Copy II with Copy I and determine the number of errors in Copy II. If there are:
no errors, mark your answer A;
1 or 2 errors, mark your answer B;
3 or 4 errors, mark your answer C;
5 or 6 errors, mark your answer D;
7 errors or more, mark your answer E.

1.   1.____
COPY I
The Commissioner, before issuing any such license, shall cause an investigation to be made of the premises named and described in such application, to determine whether all the provisions of the sanitary code, building code, state industrial code, state minimum wage law, local laws, regulations of municipal agencies, and other requirements of this article are fully observed. (Section B32-169.0 of Article 23.)

COPY II
The Commissioner, before issuing any such license shall cause an investigation to be made of the premises named and described in such application, to determine whether all the provisions of the sanitary code, bilding code, state industrial code, state minimum wage laws, local laws, regulations of municipal agencies, and other requirements of this article are fully observed. (Section E32-169.0 of Article 23.)

2.   2.____
COPY I
Among the persons who have been appointed to various agencies are John Queen, 9 West 55th Street, Brooklyn; Joseph Blount, 2497 Durward Road, Bronx; Lawrence K. Eberhardt, 3194 Bedford Street, Manhattan; Reginald L. Darcy, 1476 Allerton Drive, Bronx; and Benjamin Ledwith, 177 Greene Street, Manhattan.

2 (#2)

COPY II
Among the persons who have been appointed to various agencies are John Queen, 9 West 56th Street, Brooklyn, Joseph Blount, 2497 Dureward Road, Bronx: Lawrence K. Eberhart, 3194 Belford Street, Manhattan; Reginald L. Barcey, 1476 Allerton drive, Bronx; and Benjamin Ledwith, 177 Green Street, Manhattan.

3. 3._____

COPY I
Except as hereinafter provided, it shall be unlawful to use, store or have on hand any inflammable motion picture film in quantities greater than one standard or two sub-standard reels, or aggregating more than two thousand feet in length, or more than ten pounds in weight without the permit required by this section.

COPY II
Except as herinafter provided, it shall be unlawful to use, store or have on hand any inflamable motion picture film, in quantities greater than one standard or two substandard reels or aggregating more than two thousand feet in length, or more than ten pounds in weight without the permit required by this section.

Questions 4-6.

DIRECTIONS: Items 4 through 6 are a test of your proofreading ability. Each question consists of Copy I and Copy II. You are to assume that Copy I in each question is correct. Copy II, which is meant to be a duplicate of Copy I, may contain some typographical errors. In each question, compare Copy II with Copy I and determine the number of errors in Copy II. If there are:
no errors, mark your answer A;
1 or 2 errors, mark your answer B;
3 or 4 errors, mark your answer C;
5 or 6 errors or more, mark your answer D;

4. 4._____

COPY I
It shall be unlawful to install wires or appliances for electric light, heat or power, operating at a potential in excess of seven hundred fifty volts, in or on any part of a building, with the exception of a central station, sub-station, transformer, or switching vault, or motor room; provided, however, that the Commissioner may authorize the use of radio transmitting apparatus under special conditions.

COPY II
It shall be unlawful to install wires or appliances for electric light, heat or power, operating at a potential in excess of seven hundred fifty volts, in or on any part of a building, with the exception of a central station, sub-station, transformer, or switching vault, or motor room, provided, however, that the Commissioner may authorize the use of radio transmitting apperatus under special conditions.

5.

COPY I
The grand total debt service for the fiscal year 2006-27 amounts to $350,563,718.63, as compared with $309,561,347.27 for the current fiscal year, or an increase of $41,002,371.36. The amount payable from other sources in 2006-07 shows an increase of $13,264,165.47, resulting in an increase of $27,733,205.89 payable from tax levy funds.

COPY II
The grand total debt service for the fiscal year 2006-07 amounts to $350,568,718.63, as compared with $309,561,347.27 for the current fiscel year, or an increase of $41,002,371.36. The amount payable from other sources in 2006-07 show an increase of $13,264,165.47 resulting in an increase of $27,733,295.89 payable from tax levy funds.

6.

COPY I
The following site proposed for the new building is approximately rectangular in shape and comprises an entire block, having frontages of about 721 feet on 16th Road, 200 feet on 157th feet, 721 on 17th Avenue and 200 feet on 154th Street, with a gross area of about 144,350 square feet. The 2006-07 assessed valuation is $28,700,000 of which $6,000,000 is for improvements.

COPY II
The following site proposed for the new building is approximately rectangular in shape and comprises an entire block, having frontage of about 721 feet on 16th Road, 200 feet on 157th Street on 17th Avenue, and 200 feet on 134th Street, with a gross area of about 114,350 square feet. The 2006-07 assessed valuation is $28,700,000 of which $6,000,000 is for improvements.

KEY (CORRECT ANSWERS)

1. D   4. B
2. E   5. D
3. E   6. C

TEST 3

DIRECTIONS: Each question or incomplete statement is followed by several suggested answers or completions. Select the one that BEST answers the question or completes the statement. *PRINT THE LETTER OF THE CORRECT ANSWER IN THE SPACE AT THE RIGHT.*

Questions 1-8.

DIRECTIONS: Each of the questions numbered 1 through 8 consists of three sets of names and name codes. In each question, the two names and name codes on the same line are supposed to be exactly the same.
Look carefully at each set of names and cods and mark your answer
A. if there are mistakes in all three sets
B. if there are mistakes in two of the sets
C. if there is a mistake in only one set
D. if there are no mistakes in any of the sets

SAMPLE QUESTION

The following sample question is given to help you understand the procedure.

    Macabe, John N. – V53162   Macade, John N. – V53162
    Howard, Joan S. – J24791   Howard, Joan S. – J24791
    Ware, Susan B. – A45068   Ware, Susan B. – A45968

In the above sample question, the names and name codes of the first set are not exactly the same because of the spelling of the last name (Macabe – Macade). The names and name codes of the second set are exactly the same. The names and name codes of the third set are not exactly the same because the two name codes are different (A45068 – A45968). Since there are mistakes in only 2 of the sets, the answer to the sample question is B.

1. Powell, Michael C. – 78537F   Powell, Michael C. – 78537F   1.____
   Martinez, Pablo J. – 24435P   Martinez, Pablo J. – 24435P
   MacBane, Eliot M. – 98674E   MacBane, Eliot M. – 98674E

2. Fitz-Kramer Machines, Inc. – 259090   Fitz-Kramer Machines, Inc. – 259090   2.____
   Marvel Cleaning Service – 482657   Marvel Cleaning Service – 482657
   Donato, Carl G. – 637418   Danato, Carl G. - 687418

3. Martin Davison Trading Corp –   Martin Davidson Trading Corp. –   3.____
     43108T   43108T
   Cotwald Lighting Fixtures -76065L   Cotwald Lighting Fixtures – 70056L
   R. Crawford Plumbers – 23157C   R. Crawford Plumbers – 23157G

4. Fraiman Engineering Corp. – M4773   Friaman Engineering Corp. – M4773   4.____
   Neuman, Walter B. – N7745   Neumen, Walter B. – N7745
   Pierce, Eric M. – W6304   Pierce, Eric M. – W6304

5. Constable, Eugene – B64837　　　　Comstable, Eugene – B6437　　　　5.____
   Derrick, Paul – H27119　　　　　　　Derrik, Paul – H27119
   Heller, Karen – S4966　　　　　　　　Heller, Karen – S46906

6. Hernando Delivery Service Co. -　　Hernando Delivery Service Co. –　　6.____
   D7456　　　　　　　　　　　　　　　　D7456
   Barettz Electrical Supplies -　　　　Barettz Electrical Supplies –
   N5392　　　　　　　　　　　　　　　　N5392
   Tanner, Abraham – M4798　　　　　Tanner, Abraham – M4798

7. Kalin Associates – R38641　　　　　Kaline Associates – R38641　　　　7.____
   Sealey, Robert E. – P63533　　　　　Sealey, Robert E. – P63553
   Seals! Office Furniture – R36742　　Seals! Office Furniture – R36742

8. Janowsky, Philip M. – 742213　　　Janowsky, Philip M. – 742213　　　8.____
   Hansen, Thomas H. – 934816　　　　Hanson, Thomas H. – 934816
   L. Lester and Son Inc. – 294568　　　L. Lester and Son Inc. - 294568

Questions 9-13.

DIRECTIONS: Each of the questions numbered 9 through 13 consists of three sets of names and building codes. In each question, the two names and building codes on the same line are supposed to be exactly the same.
If you find an error or errors on only one of the sets in the question, mark your answer A; any two of the sets in the question, mark your answer B; all three of the sets in the question, mark your answer C; none of the sets, mark your answer D.

SAMPLE QUESTION

Column I　　　　　　　　　　　　　　Column II
Duvivier, Anne P. – X52714　　　　　Duviver, Anne P. – X52714
Dyrborg, Alfred – B4217　　　　　　　Dyrborg, Alfred – B4267
Dymnick, JoAnne – P482596　　　　　Dymnick, JoAnne – P482596

In the above sample question, the first set of names and building codes is not exactly the same because the last names are spelled differently (Duvivier – Duviver). The second set of names and building codes is not exactly the same because the building codes are different (B4217 – B4267). The third set of names and building codes is exactly the same. Since there are mistakes in two of the sets of names and building codes, the answer to the sample question is B.

Now answer the questions using the same procedure.

Column I　　　　　　　　　　　　　　Column II
9. Lautmann, Gerald G. – C2483　　　Lautmann, Gerald C. – C2483　　　9.____
   Lawlor, Michael – W44639　　　　　Lawler, Michael – W44639
   Lawrence, John J. – H1358　　　　　Lawrence, John J. – H1358

Column I | Column II

10. Mittmann, Howard – J4113
    Mitchell, William T. – M75271
    Milan, T. Thomas – Q67553

    Mittmann, Howard – J4113
    Mitchell, William T. – M75721
    Milan, T. Thomas – Q67553

    10._____

11. Quarles, Vincent – J34760
    Quinn, Alan N. – S38813
    Quinones, Peter W. – B87467

    Quarles, Vincent – J34760
    Quinn, Alan N. – S38813
    Quinones, Peter W. – B87467

    11._____

12. Daniels, Harold H. – A26554
    Dantzler, Richard – C35780
    Davidson, Martina – E62901

    Daniels, Harold H – A26544
    Dantzler, Richard – 035780
    Davidson, Martin – E62901

    12._____

13. Graham, Cecil J. – I20244
    Granger, Deborah – T86211
    Grant, Charles L. – G5788

    Graham, Cecil J. – I20244
    Granger, Deborah – T86211
    Grant, Charles L. – G5788

    13._____

KEY (CORRECT ANSWERS)

1.	D	6.	D	11.	D
2.	C	7.	B	12.	C
3.	A	8.	C	13.	D
4.	B	9.	B		
5.	A	10.	A		

TEST 4

DIRECTIONS: In Questions 1 through 10 there are five pairs of numbers or letters and numbers. Compare each pair and decide how many pairs are exactly alike. *PRINT THE LETTER OF THE CORRECT ANSWER IN THE SPACE AT THE RIGHT.*
  A. if only one pair is exactly alike
  B. if only two pairs are exactly alike
  C. if only three pairs are exactly alike
  D. if only four pairs are exactly alike
  E. if all five pairs are exactly alike.

1. 73-F.....F-73
   F-7373.....F-7373
   F-733.....337-F
   FF-73.....FF-73
   373-FF.....337-FF   1.____

2. 0-17158.....0-17158
   0-11758.....0-11758
   0-71518.....0-71518
   0-15817.....0-15817   2.____

3. 1A-7908.....1A-7908
   71-891.....7A-891
   9A-7018.....9A-7081
   7A-8901.....7A-8091
   1A-9078.....1A-9708   3.____

4. 2V-6426.....2V-6246
   2V-6426.....2N-6426
   2V-6462.....2V-6562
   2N-6246.....2N-6246
   2N-6624.....2N-6624   4.____

5. 3NY-56.....3NY-65
   6NY-3566.....3NY-3566
   3NY-5663.....5NY-3663
   5NY-356.....3NY-356
   5NY-6536.....5NY-6536   5.____

6. COB-065.....COB-065
   LBC-650.....LBC-650
   CDB-056.....COB-065
   BCL-506.....BCL-506
   DLB-560.....DLB-560   6.____

7. 4KQ-9130.....4KQ-9130
   4KQ-9031.....4KQ-9301
   4KQ-9013.....4KQ-9013
   4KQ-9310.....4KQ-9130
   4KQ-9301.....4KQ-9301   7.____

8. MK-89.....MK-98
   MSK-998.....MSK-998
   SMK-899.....SMK-899
   98-MK.....89-MK
   MOSK.....MOKS   8.____

9. 8MD-2104.....SMD-2014
   814-MD.....814-MD
   MD-281.....MD-481
   2MD-8140.....2MD-8140
   4MD-8201.....4MD-8201   9.____

10. 161-035.....161-035
    315-160.....315-160
    165-301.....165-301
    150-316.....150-316
    131-650.....131-650   10.____

KEY (CORRECT ANSWERS)

1.	B	6.	D
2.	E	7.	D
3.	B	8.	B
4.	C	9.	C
5.	A	10.	E

TEST 5

DIRECTIONS: Each question or incomplete statement is followed by several suggested answers or completions. Select the one that BEST answers the question or completes the statement. *PRINT THE LETTER OF THE CORRECT ANSWER IN THE SPACE AT THE RIGHT.*

Questions -5.

DIRECTIONS: Questions 1 through 5, inclusive, consist of groups of four displays representing license identification plates. Examine each group of plates and determine the number of plates in each group which are identical. Mark your answer sheets as follows:
  If only two plates are identical, mark answer A.
  If only three plates are identical, mark answer B.
  If all four plates are identical, mark answer C.
  If the plates are all different, mark answer D.

EXAMPLE
ABC123 BCD123 ABC123 BCD235

Since only two plates are identical, the first and third, the correct answer is A.

1.	PBV839	PVB839	PVB839	PVB839	1.____
2.	WTX083	WTX083	WTX083	WTX083	2.____
3.	B73609	D73906	BD7396	BD7906	3.____
4.	AK7423	AK7423	AK1423	A81324	4.____
5.	583Y10	683Y10	583701	583710	5.____

Questions 6-10.

DIRECTIONS: Questions 6 through 10 consist of groups of numbers and letters similar to those which might appear on license plates. Each group of numbers and letters will be called a license identification. Choose the license identification lettered A, B, C, or D that EXACTLY matches the license identification shown next to the question number.

SAMPLE
NY 1977
ABC-123

A. NY 1976   B. NY 1977   C. NY 1977   D. NY 1977
   ABC-123   ABC-132   CBA-123   ABC-123

The license identification given is NY 1977.
ABC-123
The only choice that exactly matches it is the license identification next to the letter D. The correct answer is therefore D.

6. NY 1976
QLT-781

   A. NJ 1976 QLT-781
   B. NY 1975 QLT-781
   C. NY 1976 QLT-781
   D. NY 1977 QLT-781

6.____

7. FLA 1977
2-7LT58J

   A. FLA 1977 2-7TL58J
   B. FLA 1977 2-7LTJ58
   C. FLA 1977 2-7LT58J
   D. LA 1977 2-7LT58J

7.____

8. NY 1975
OQC383

   A. NY 1975 OQC383
   B. NY 1975 OQC833
   C. NY 1975 QCQ383
   D. NY 1977 OCQ383

8.____

9. MASS 1977
B-8DK02

   A. MISS 1977 B-8DK02
   B. MASS 1977 B-8DK02
   C. MASS 1976 B-8DK02
   D. MASS 1977 B-80KD2

9.____

10. NY 1976
ZV0586

   A. NY 1976 2V-0586
   B. NY 1977 ZV0586
   C. NY 1975 ZV0586
   D. NY 1976 ZU0586

10.____

KEY (CORRECT ANSWERS)

1.	B	6.	C
2.	C	7.	C
3.	D	8.	A
4.	A	9.	B
5.	A	10.	C

TEST 6

DIRECTIONS: Assume that each of the capital letters in the table below represent the name of an employee enrolled in the city employees' retirement system. The number directly beneath the letter represents the agency for which the employee works, and the small letter directly beneath represents the code for the employee's account.

Name of Employee	L	O	T	Q	A	M	R	N	C
Agency	3	4	5	9	8	7	2	1	6
Account Code	r	f	b	i	d	t	g	e	n

In each of the following questions 1 through 3, the agency code numbers and the account code letters in Columns 2 and 3 should correspond to the capital letters in Column 1 and should be in the same consecutive order. For each question, look at each column carefully and mark your answer as follows:
If there are one or more errors in Column 2 only, mark your answer A.
If there are one or more errors in Column 3 only, mark your answer B.
If there are one or more errors in Column 2 and one or more errors in Column 3, mark your answer C.
If there are NO errors in either column, mark your answer D.
The following sample question is given to help you understand the procedure.

Column 1   Column 2   Column 3
TQLMOC   583746   birtfn

In Column 2, the second agency code number (corresponding to letter Q) should be "9", not "8". Column 3 is coded correctly to Column 1. Since there is an error only in Column 2, the correct answer is A.

	Column 1	Column 2	Column 3	
1.	QLNRCA	931268	iregnd	1._____
2.	NRMOTC	127546	egftbn	2._____
3.	RCTALM	265837	gndbrt	3._____

KEY (CORRECT ANSWERS)

1. D
2. C
3. B

NAME AND NUMBER COMPARISONS

COMMENTARY

This test seeks to measure your ability and disposition to do a job carefully and accurately, your attention to exactness and preciseness of detail, your alertness and versatility in discerning similarities and differences between things, and your power in systematically handling written language symbols.

It is actually a test of your ability to do academic and/or clerical work, using the basic elements of verbal (qualitative) and mathematical (quantitative) learning—words and numbers.

EXAMINATION SECTION

TEST 1

DIRECTIONS: In each line across the page there are three names or numbers that are much alike. Compare the three names or numbers and decide which ones are exactly alike. *PRINT IN THE SPACE AT THE RIGHT THE LETTER:*
    A. if all THREE names or numbers are exactly alike
    B. if only the FIRST and SECOND names or numbers are ALIKE
    C. if only the FIRST and THIRD names or numbers are alike
    D. if only the SECOND or THIRD names or numbers are alike
    E. if ALL THREE names or numbers are DIFFERENT

1. Davis Hazen   David Hozen   David Hazen   1.____
2. Lois Appel   Lois Appel   Lois Apfel   2.____
3. June Allan   Jane Allan   Jane Allan   3.____
4. 10235   10235   10235   4.____
5. 32614   32164   32614   5.____

TEST 2

1. 2395890   2395890   2395890   1.____
2. 1926341   1926347   1926314   2.____
3. E. Owens McVey   E. Owen McVey   E. Owen McVay   3.____
4. Emily Neal Rouse   Emily Neal Rowse   Emily Neal Rowse   4.____
5. H. Merritt Audubon   H. Merriott Audubon   H. Merritt Audubon   5.____

TEST 3

1. 6219354	6219354	6219354	1.____
2. 231793	2312793	2312793	2.____
3. 1065407	1065407	1065047	3.____
4. Francis Ransdell	Frances Ramsdell	Francis Ramsdell	4.____
5. Cornelius Detwiler	Cornelius Detwiler	Cornelius Detwiler	5.____

TEST 4

1. 6452054	6452564	6542054	1.____
2. 8501268	8501268	8501286	2.____
3. Ella Burk Newham	Ella Burk Newnham	Elena Burk Newnham	3.____
4. Jno. K. Ravencroft	Jno. H. Ravencroft	Jno. H. Ravencoft	4.____
5. Martin Wills Pullen	Martin Wills Pulen	Martin Wills Pullen	5.____

TEST 5

1. 3457988	3457986	3457986	1.____
2. 4695682	4695862	4695682	2.____
3. Stricklund Kaneydy	Sticklund Kanedy	Stricklund Kanedy	3.____
4. Joy Harlor Witner	Joy Harloe Witner	Joy Harloe Witner	4.____
5. R.M.O. Uberroth	R.M.O. Uberroth	R.N.O. Uberroth	5.____

TEST 6

1. 1592514	1592574	1592574	1.____
2. 2010202	2010202	2010220	2.____
3. 6177396	6177936	6177396	3.____
4. Drusilla S. Ridgeley	Drusilla S. Ridgeley	Drusilla S. Ridgeley	4.____
5. Andrei I. Tooumantzev	Andrei I. Tourmantzev	Andrei I. Toumantzov	5.____

TEST 7

1. 5261383	5261383	5261338	1.____
2. 8125690	8126690	8125609	2.____
3. W.E. Johnston	W.E. Johnson	W.E. Johnson	3.____
4. Vergil L. Muller	Vergil L. Muller	Vergil L. Muller	4.____
5. Atherton R. Warde	Asheton R. Warde	Atherton P. Warde	5.____

TEST 8

1. 013469.5	023469.5	02346.95	1.____
2. 33376	333766	333766	2.____
3. Ling-Temco-Vought	Ling-Tenco-Vought	Ling-Temco Vought	3.____
4. Lorilard Corp.	Lorillard Corp.	Lorrilard Corp.	4.____
5. American Agronomics Corporation	American Agronomics Corporation	American Agronomic Corporation	5.____

TEST 9

1.	436592864	436592864	436592864	1.____
2.	197765123	197755123	197755123	2.____
3.	Dewaay Cortvriendt International S.A.	Deway Cortvriendt International S.A.	Deway Corturiendt International S.A.	3.____
4.	Crèdit Lyonnais	Crèdit Lyonnais	Crèdit Lyonais	4.____
5.	Algemene Bank Nederland N.V.	Algamene Bank Nederland N.V.	Algemene Bank Naderland N.V.	5.____

TEST 10

1.	00032572	0.0032572	00032522	1.____
2.	399745	399745	398745	2.____
3.	Banca Privata Finanziaria S.p.A.	Banca Privata Finanzaria S.P.A.	Banca Privata Finanziaria S.P.A.	3.____
4.	Eastman Dillon, Union Securities & Co.	Eastman Dillon, Union Securities Co.	Eastman Dillon, Union Securities & Co.	4.____
5.	Arnhold and S. Bleichroeder, Inc.	Arnhold & S. Bleichroeder, Inc.	Arnold and S. Bleichroeder, Inc.	5.____

TEST 11

DIRECTIONS: Answer the questions below on the basis of the following instructions: For each such numbered set of names, addresses, and numbers listed in Columns I and II, select your answer from the following options:
  A. The names in Columns I and II are different
  B. The addresses in Columns I and II are different
  C. The numbers in Columns I and II are different
  D. The names, addresses and numbers are identical

1. Francis Jones
   62 Stately Avenue
   96-12446

   Francis Jones
   62 Stately Avenue
   96-21446

   1.____

2. Julio Montez
   19 Ponderosa Road
   56-73161

   Julio Montez
   19 Ponderosa Road
   56-71361

   2.____

3. Mary Mitchell
   2314 Melbourne Drive
   68-92172

   Mary Mitchell
   2314 Melbourne Drive
   68-92172

   3.____

4. Harry Patterson
   25 Dunne Street
   14-33430

   Harry Patterson
   25 Dunne Street
   14-34330

   4.____

5. Patrick Murphy
   171 West Hosmer Street
   93-81214

   Patrick Murphy
   171 West Hosmer Street
   93-18214

   5.____

TEST 12

1. August Schultz
   816 St. Clair Avenue
   53-40149

   August Schultz
   816 St. Claire Avenue
   53-40149

   1.____

2. George Taft
   72 Runnymede Street
   47-04033

   George Taft
   72 Runnymede Street
   47-04023

   2.____

3. Angus Henderson
   1418 Madison Street
   81-76375

   Angus Henderson
   1418 Madison Street
   81-76375

   3.____

4. Carolyn Mazur
   12 Rivenlew Road
   38-99615

   Carolyn Mazur
   12 Rivervane Road
   38-99615

   4.____

5. Adele Russell
   1725 Lansing Lane
   72-91962

   Adela Russell
   1725 Lansing Lane
   72-91962

   5.____

TEST 13

DIRECTIONS: The following questions are based on the instructions given below. In each of the following questions, the 3-line name and address in Column I is the master-list entry, and the 3-line entry in Column II is the information to be checked against the master list.
If there is one line that is NOT exactly alike, mark your answer A.
If there are two lines NOT exactly alike, mark your answer B.
If there are three lines NOT exactly alike, mark your answer C.
If the lines ALL are exactly alike, mark your answer D.

1. Jerome A. Jackson　　　　　　　　Jerome A. Johnson　　　　　　1.____
   1243 14th Avenue　　　　　　　　　1234 14th Avenue
   New York, N.Y. 10023　　　　　　　New York, N.Y. 10023

2. Sophie Strachtheim　　　　　　　　Sophie Strachtheim　　　　　　2.____
   33-28 Connecticut Ave.　　　　　　 33-28 Connecticut Ave.
   Far Rockaway, N.Y. 11697　　　　　Far Rockaway, N.Y. 11697

3. Elisabeth NT. Gorrell　　　　　　　Elizabeth NT. Correll　　　　　3.____
   256 Exchange St　　　　　　　　　256 Exchange St.
   New York, N.Y. 10013　　　　　　　New York, N.Y. 10013

4. Maria J. Gonzalez　　　　　　　　Maria J. Gonzalez　　　　　　　4.____
   7516 E. Sheepshead Rd.　　　　　　7516 N. Shepshead Rd.
   Brooklyn, N.Y. 11240　　　　　　　Brooklyn, N.Y. 11240

5. Leslie B. Brautenweiler　　　　　　Leslie B. Brautenwieler　　　　5.____
   21-57A Seller Terr.　　　　　　　　21-75ASeiler Terr.
   Flushing, N.Y. 11367　　　　　　　Flushing, N.J. 11367

KEY (CORRECT ANSWERS)

TEST 1	TEST 2	TEST 3	TEST 4	TEST 5	TEST 6	TEST 7
1. E	1. A	1. A	1. E	1. D	1. D	1. B
2. B	2. E	2. A	2. B	2. C	2. B	2. E
3. D	3. E	3. B	3. E	3. E	3. C	3. D
4. A	4. D	4. E	4. E	4. D	4. A	4. A
5. C	5. C	5. A	5. C	5. B	5. E	5. E

TEST 8	TEST 9	TEST 10	TEST 11	TEST 12	TEST 13
1. E	1. A	1. E	1. C	1. B	1. B
2. D	2. D	2. B	2. C	2. C	2. D
3. E	3. E	3. E	3. D	3. D	3. A
4. E	4. E	4. C	4. C	4. B	4. A
5. B	5. E	5. E	5. C	5. A	5. C

NAME AND NUMBER COMPARISONS

COMMENTARY

This test seeks to measure your ability and disposition to do a job carefully and accurately, your attention to exactness and preciseness of detail, your alertness and versatility in discerning similarities and differences between things, and your power in systematically handling written language symbols.

It is actually a test of your ability to do academic and/or clerical work, using the basic elements of verbal (qualitative) and mathematical (quantitative) learning—words and numbers.

EXAMINATION SECTION

TEST 1

DIRECTIONS: Questions 1 through 6 consist of sets of names and addresses. In each question, the name and address in Column II should be an exact copy of the name and address in Column II. *PRINT IN THE SPACE AT THE RIGHT THE LETTER*
    A. if there is a mistake only in the name
    B. if there is a mistake only in the address
    C. if there is a mistake in both name and address
    D. If there is no mistake in either name or address

SAMPLE:
Michael Filbert	Michael Filbert
456 Reade Street	644 Reade Street
New York, N.Y. 10013	New York, N.Y. 10013

Since there is a mistake only in the address, the answer is B.

1. Esta Wong
141 West 68 St.
New York, N.Y. 10023

   Esta Wang
141 West 68 St.
New York, N.Y. 10023

   1.____

2. Dr. Alberto Grosso
3475 12th Avenue
Brooklyn, N.Y. 11218

   Dr. Alberto Grosso
3475 12th Avenue
Brooklyn, N.Y. 11218

   2.____

3. Mrs. Ruth Bortlas
482 Theresa Ct.
Far Rockaway, N.Y. 11691

   Ms. Ruth Bortias
482 Theresa Ct.
Far Rockaway, N.Y. 11169

   3.____

4. Mr. and Mrs. Howard Fox
2301 Sedgwick Ave.
Bronx, N.Y. 10468

   Mr. and Mrs. Howard Fox
231 Sedgwick Ave.
Bronx, N.Y. 10468

   4.____

5. Miss Marjorie Black
223 East 23 Street
New York, N.Y. 10010

   Miss Margorie Black
223 East 23 Street
New York, N.Y. 10010

   5.____

6. Michelle Herman   Michelle Hermann   6.____
    806 Valley Rd.   806 Valley Dr.
    Old Tappan, N.J. 07675   Old Tappan, N.J. 07675

KEY (CORRECT ANSWERS)

1. A
2. D
3. C
4. B
5. A
6. C

TEST 2

DIRECTIONS: Questions 1 through 6 consist of sets of names and addresses. In each question, the name and address in Column II should be an exact copy of the name and address in Column II. *PRINT IN THE SPACE AT THE RIGHT THE LETTER*
- A. if there is a mistake only in the name
- B. if there is a mistake only in the address
- C. if there is a mistake in both name and address
- D. If there is no mistake in either name or address

1. Ms. Joan Kelly
   313 Franklin Ave.
   Brooklyn, N.Y. 11202

   Ms. Joan Kielly
   318 Franklin Ave.
   Brooklyn, N.Y. 11202

   1.____

2. Mrs. Eileen Engel
   47-24 86 Road
   Queens, N.Y. 11122

   Mrs. Ellen Engel
   47-24 86 Road
   Queens, N.Y. 11122

   2.____

3. Marcia Michaels
   213 E. 81 St.
   New York, N.Y. 10012

   Marcia Michaels
   213 E. 81 St.
   New York, N.Y. 10012

   3.____

4. Rev. Edward J. Smyth
   1401 Brandeis Street
   San Francisco, Calif. 96201

   Rev. Edward J. Smyth
   1401 Brandies Street
   San Francisco, Calif. 96201

   4.____

5. Alicia Rodriguez
   24-68 81 St.
   Elmhurst, N.Y. 11122

   Alicia Rodriquez
   2468 81 St.
   Elmhurst, N.Y. 11122

   5.____

6. Ernest Eissemann
   21 Columbia St.
   New York, N.Y. 10007

   Ernest Eisermann
   21 Columbia St.
   New York, N.Y. 10007

   6.____

KEY (CORRECT ANSWERS)

1. C
2. A
3. D
4. B
5. C
6. A

TEST 3

DIRECTIONS: Questions 1 through 8 consist of names, locations, and telephone numbers. In each question, the name, location and number in Column II should be an exact copy of the name, location, and number in Column I. *PRINT IN THE SPACE AT THE RIGHT THE LETTER*
- A. if there is a mistake in one line only
- B. if there is a mistake in two lines only
- C. if there is a mistake in three lines only
- D. if there are no mistakes in any of the lines

1. Ruth Lang
   EAM Bldg., Room C101
   625-2000, ext. 765

   Ruth Lang
   EAM Bldg., Room C110
   625-2000, ext. 765
   1.____

2. Anne Marie Ionozzi
   Investigations, Room 827
   576-4000, ext. 832

   Anna Marie Ionozzi
   Investigation, Room 827
   566-4000, ext. 832
   2.____

3. Willard Jameson
   Fm C Bldg. Room 687
   454-3010

   Willard Jamieson
   Fm C Bldg. Room 687
   454-3010
   3.____

4. Joanne Zimmermann
   Bldg. SW, Room 314
   532-4601

   Joanne Zimmermann
   Bldg. SW, Room 314
   532-4601
   4.____

5. Carlyle Whetstone
   Payroll Division-A, Room 212A
   262-5000, ext. 471

   Caryle Whetstone
   Payroll Division-A, Room 212A
   262-5000, ext. 417
   5.____

6. Kenneth Chiang
   Legal Council, Room 9745
   (201) 416-9100, ext. 17

   Kenneth Chiang
   Legal Counsel, Room 9745
   (201) 416-9100, ext. 17
   6.____

7. Ethel Koenig
   Personnel Services Div, Rm 433
   635-7572

   Ethel Hoenig
   Personal Services Div, Rm 433
   635-7527
   7.____

8. Joyce Ehrhardt
   Office of Administrator, Rm W56
   387-8706

   Joyce Ehrhart
   Office of Administrator, Rm W56
   387-7806
   8.____

KEY (CORRECT ANSWERS)

1. A   6. A
2. C   7. C
3. A   8. B
4. D
5. B

TEST 4

DIRECTIONS: Each of Questions 1 through 10 gives the identification number and name of a person who has received treatment at a certain hospital. You are to choose the option (A, B, C, or D) which has EXACTLY the same number and name as those given in the question.

SAMPLE QUESTION:
123765 Frank Y. Jones
   A. 123675 Frank Y. Jones
   B. 123765 Frank T. Jones
   C. 123765 Frank Y. Jones
   D. 123765 Frank Y. Jones

The correct answer is D, because it is the only option showing the identification number and name exactly as they are in the sample question.

1. 754898 Diane Malloy
   A. 745898 Diane Malloy   B. 754898 Dion Malloy
   C. 754898 Diane Malloy   D. 754898 Diane Maloy

2. 661818 Ferdinand Figueroa
   A. 661818 Ferdinand Figueroa   B. 661618 Ferdinand Figueroa
   C. 661818 Ferdnand Figueroa   D. 661818 Ferdinand Figueroa

3. 100101 Norman D. Braustein
   A. 100101 Norman D. Braustein   B. 101001 Norman D. Braustein
   C. 100101 Norman P. Braustien   D. 100101 Norman D. Bruastein

4. 838696 Robert Kittredge
   A. 838969 Robert Kittredge   B. 838696 Robert Kittredge
   C. 388696 Robert Kittredge   D. 838696 Robert Kittridge

5. 243716 Abraham Soletsky
   A. 243716 Abrahm Soletsky   B. 243716 Abraham Solestky
   C. 243176 Abraham Soletsky   D. 243716 Abraham Soletsky

6. 981121 Phillip M. Maas
   A. 981121 Phillip M. Mass   B. 981211 Phillip M. Maas
   C. 981121 Phillip M. Maas   D. 981121 Phillip N. Maas

7. 786556 George Macalusso
   A. 785656 George Macalusso   B. 786556 George Macalusso
   C. 786556 George Maculusso   D. 786556 George Macluasso

8. 639472 Eugene Weber
   A. 639472 Eugene Weber   B. 639472 Eugene Webre
   C. 693472 Eugene Weber   D. 639742 Eugene Weber

9. 724936 John J. Lomonaco   9.____
   A. 724936 John J. Lomanoco   B. 724396 John L. Lomonaco
   C. 7224936 John J. Lomonaco   D. 724936 John J. Lamonaco

10. 899868 Michael Schnitzer   10.____
   A. 899868 Micheal Schnitzer   B. 898968 Michael Schnizter
   C. 899688 Michael Schnitzer   D. 899868 Michael Schnitzer

KEY (CORRECT ANSWERS)

1.	C	6.	C
2.	D	7.	B
3.	A	8.	A
4.	B	9.	C
5.	D	10.	D

EXAMINATION SECTION
TEST 1

DIRECTIONS: Each question or incomplete statement is followed by several suggested answers or completions. Select the one that BEST answers the question or completes the statement. *PRINT THE LETTER OF THE CORRECT ANSWER IN THE SPACE AT THE RIGHT.*

1. The detection of counterfeiting and the apprehension of counterfeiters Is PRIMARILY the responsibility of the

   A. Federal Bureau of Investigation
   B. United States Secret Service
   C. Federal Reserve Board
   D. National Security Council

2. The term *legal tender* applies to

   A. a check, legally endorsed, and intended for deposit only
   B. money which may lawfully be used in the payment of debts
   C. foreign money whose rate of exchange is set by law
   D. uncoined gold or silver in the form of bullion bars

Questions 3-4.

DIRECTIONS: Questions 3 and 4 are to be answered SOLELY on the basis of the information contained in the following statement:

When a design for a new bank note of the Federal Government has been prepared by the Bureau of Engraving and Printing and has been approved by the Secretary of the Treasury, the engravers begin the work of cutting the design in steel. No one engraver does all the work. Each man is a specialist. One works only on portraits, another on lettering, another on scroll work, and so on. Each engraver, with a steel tool known as a graver, and aided by a powerful magnifying glass, carefully carves his portion of the design into the steel. He knows that one false cut or a slip of his tool, or one miscalculation of width or depth of line, may destroy the merit of his work. A single mistake means that months or weeks of labor will have been in vain. The Bureau is proud of the fact that no counterfeiter ever has duplicated the excellent work of its expert engravers.

3. According to the above statement, each engraver in the Bureau of Engraving and Printing

   A. must be approved by the Secretary of the Treasury before he can begin work on the design for a new bank note
   B. is responsible for engraving a complete design of a new bank note himself
   C. designs new bank notes and submits them for approval to the Secretary of the Treasury
   D. performs only a specific part of the work of engraving a design for a new bank note

4. According to the above statement,

A. an engraver's tools are not available to a counterfeiter
B. mistakes made in engraving a design can be corrected immediately with little delay in the work of the Bureau
C. the skilled work of the engravers has not been successfully reproduced by counterfeiters
D. careful carving and cutting by the engravers is essential to prevent damage to equipment

5. The public lays down the rules governing the type of service that it expects to be given. These rules are expressed partly in laws and partly in public opinion, which at any time may be made into law. Private business and government departments have, and always have had, the task of giving the public what it expects, a task which has lately come to be called public relations. According to the above statement,

    A. government departments have the task of serving the public as it wishes to be served
    B. private firms emphasize public relations more than public agencies do
    C. the rules for giving the public the service it expects are all eventually made into laws
    D. the task of public relations is to inform the public about the work of government departments

6. Certain personal qualities are required of an employee who is to perform a particular assignment efficiently. Since each employee possesses different qualities, experience indicates that it is important to seek and select the employee who possesses the personal qualities required for the particular assignment.
According to the above statement,

    A. the personal qualities of an employee should be changed to fit a particular assignment
    B. personal qualities are more important than experience in the performance of an assignment
    C. an assignment should be changed to fit the personal qualities of the employee assigned to it
    D. the employee selected for an assignment should have the personal qualities needed to perform it

7. A cashier has to make many arithmetic calculations in connection with his work. Skill in arithmetic comes readily with practice; no special talent is needed.
On the basis of the above statement, it is MOST accurate to state that

    A. the most important part of a cashier's job is to make calculations
    B. few cashiers have the special ability needed to handle arithmetic problems easily
    C. without special talent, cashiers cannot learn to do the calculations they are required to do in their work
    D. a cashier can, with practice, learn to handle the computations he is required to make

8. A bonded employee is much less likely to be tempted to steal money than an unbonded one, for he knows that a bonding company will prosecute him for the sake of principle, whereas an employer might not ordinarily take any action against an employee if there is no hope of recovering the stolen money.
The MOST valid implication of the above statement is that   8.____

   A. a bonded employee if often tempted to steal because he knows that his employer is protected against the loss
   B. a bonding company will attempt to find and punish the guilty employee even when the stolen money cannot be recovered
   C. an employer whose bonded employees do not steal is wasting the money spent to bond them
   D. it is wasteful for a bonding company to prosecute an employee when there is no chance of recovering the stolen money

9. The BEST of the following attitudes regarding departmental rules and regulations for a cashier to take is that they   9.____

   A. are simply a means for justifying disciplinary action taken by a supervisor
   B. are to be interpreted by each employee as he sees fit
   C. must be obeyed even if they seem unreasonable in some cases
   D. should be read and studied but may be ignored whenever an employee feels it is necessary to do so

10. It is MOST important for a cashier who is assigned to perform a lengthy monotonous task to   10.____

    A. perform this task before doing his other work
    B. ask another cashier to assist him to dispose of the task quickly
    C. perform this task only when his other work has been completed
    D. take measures to prevent mistakes in performing this task

11. Although accuracy and speed are both important for a cashier in the performance of his work, accuracy should be considered more important MAINLY because   11.____

    A. most supervisors insist on accurate work
    B. much time is lost in correcting errors
    C. a rapid rate of work cannot be maintained for any length of time
    D. speedy workers are usually inaccurate

12. Of the following, the CHIEF reason why a cashier should not be late to work in the morning is that   12.____

    A. he will probably be penalized for his lateness
    B. the work of his unit may be delayed because of his tardiness
    C. he will set a bad example for the other employees to follow
    D. a poor attendance record may affect his supervisor's evaluation of his work

13. A cashier who handles large quantities of currency should know that the term *Silver Certificate* usually referred to   13.____

    A. a receipt for silver bars deposited with a bank
    B. a form of paper money that is acceptable only for the payment of non-business debts

C. a certificate issued by a refiner of silver metal to show the purity of his product
D. a form of paper money that is backed by silver owned by the United States Government

14. There are 12 consecutively numbered Federal Reserve Districts, each having as its symbol a number and the corresponding letter of the alphabet. The Federal Reserve Bank in each district has the same symbol as that of its district. For example, the Federal Reserve Bank of Boston is in the first Federal Reserve District and has as its symbol the number *1* and the letter *A*. The other districts, in numerical order, are New York, Philadelphia, Cleveland, Richmond, Atlanta, Chicago, St. Louis, Minneapolis, Kansas City, Dallas, and San Francisco.
According to the above statement, the Federal Reserve Bank of Philadelphia is represented by the

A. number *2* and the letter *B*
B. number *2* and the letter *C*
C. number *3* and the letter *B*
D. number *3* and the letter *C*

15. Of the following, the MOST important reason for a cashier to know the portraits that appear on each denomination of paper currency is that

A. he will be able to count bills merely by looking at the portraits
B. familiarity with portraits may help him to identify a counterfeit bill that has had its denomination changed from a lower to a higher amount
C. a greater knowledge of currency may help increase his promotional opportunities
D. the United States Treasury Department sometimes changes the portraits appearing on various currency denominations

16. The one of the following which is a characteristic of a genuine bill is that its portrait

A. has a fine screen of regular lines in its background
B. has irregular and broken lines in its background
C. has a very dark blue background
D. merges into the background

17. Of the following characteristics, the one that is LEAST helpful in deciding whether a bill is counterfeit is that the

A. portrait is dull, smudgy or scratchy
B. serial numbers are unevenly spaced
C. geometric lathework is broken and indistinct
D. ink rubs off when the bill is rubbed on a piece of paper

18. The color of the Treasury seal and serial number on a United States Note is always

A. blue   B. gray   C. green   D. red

19. The saw teeth points on the rim of the Treasury seal on a genuine bill are generally

A. blunt and uneven   B. broken off and faded
C. indistinct   D. sharp and evenly spaced

20. If one-half of a mutilated genuine bill is sent to the Currency Redemption Division of the Treasury Department, the bill will 20.____

    A. be redeemed at one-half of its face value
    B. be redeemed at three-fifths of its face value
    C. be redeemed at its full face value
    D. not be redeemed at all

21. The color of the Treasury seal and serial number on a Federal Reserve Note is always 21.____

    A. blue   B. brown   C. green   D. red

22. The serial number on the face of a bill is printed 22.____

    A. to the right of the portrait and to the lower left of the portrait
    B. to the left of the portrait and to the lower right of the portrait
    C. directly above the portrait and directly below the portrait
    D. in the upper left corner and the lower left corner

23. The color of the check letter on the face of a bill is always 23.____

    A. black   B. blue   C. green   D. red

24. The face plate number on the face of a bill is printed in the 24.____

    A. upper left corner   B. upper right corner
    C. lower left corner   D. lower right corner

25. If three-fifths of a mutilated genuine bill is sent to the Currency Redemption Division of the Treasury Department, the bill will 25.____

    A. be redeemed at one-half of its face value
    B. be redeemed at three-fifths of its face value
    C. be redeemed at its full face value
    D. not be redeemed at all

Questions 26 - 35.

DIRECTIONS: In Column I below are listed the names of ten men and buildings. In Column II are listed seven paper currency denominations and a category *None of the above denominations*.

In questions 26 to 35, for each man or building in Column I, print in the correspondingly numbered space on your answer sheet, the capital letter preceding the denomination in Column II on which the man or building appears. If the man or building appears on none of the listed denominations, print the letter *H* in the correspondingly numbered space on your answer sheet.

COLUMN I	COLUMN II	
26. Alexander Hamilton	A. $1	26.___
27. White House	B. $2	27.___
28. Benjamin Franklin	C. $5	28.___
29. Mount Vernon	D. $10	29.___
30. Thomas Jefferson	E. $20	30.___
31. U.S. Treasury Department	F. $50	31.___
32. Andrew Jackson	G. $100	32.___
33. United States Capitol	H. None of the above denominations	33.___
34. George Washington		34.___
35. Abraham Lincoln		35.___

KEY (CORRECT ANSWERS)

1.	B	11.	B	21.	C	31.	D
2.	B	12.	B	22.	A	32.	E
3.	D	13.	D	23.	A	33.	F
4.	C	14.	D	24.	D	34.	A
5.	A	15.	B	25.	C	35.	C
6.	D	16.	A	26.	D		
7.	D	17.	D	27.	E		
8.	B	18.	D	28.	G		
9.	C	19.	D	29.	H		
10.	D	20.	A	30.	B		

TEST 2

DIRECTIONS: Each question or incomplete statement is followed by several suggested answers or completions. Select the one that BEST answers the question or completes the statement. *PRINT THE LETTER OF THE CORRECT ANSWER IN THE SPACE AT THE RIGHT.*

1. Of the following, the characteristic which describes a genuine coin MOST accurately is that the coin usually

    A. can be bent easily at the edges
    B. can be cut easily with a knife
    C. has a bell-like ring when dropped on a hard surface
    D. will not bounce when dropped on a hard surface

    1._____

2. The corrugations on the outer edge of a genuine coin are usually

    A. even and regular
    B. indistinct and blackened
    C. the same as on a counterfeit coin
    D. uneven and crooked

    2._____

3. When comparing counterfeit coins with genuine ones, most counterfeit coins usually feel

    A. greasy B. cold C. sticky D. damp

    3._____

4. A cashier who, in the course of his duties, suffers even a minor cut should have it properly cared for so that there will be no chance for infection to set in. Amputations, and even deaths, have resulted from small neglected wounds. According to the above statement, it is MOST accurate to state that

    A. a minor cut is not usually a cause for concern
    B. minor injuries are usually worse than they seem to be
    C. minor injuries should not be neglected
    D. small wounds are more dangerous than big ones

    4._____

5. Certain types of money may be photographed only with the permission of the Secretary of the Treasury. His permission is not required to photograph

    A. bills B. bonds, bills and coins
    C. coins D. either coins or bills

    5._____

6. Sometimes in the performance of his duties, a cashier must act alone, without advice from his superior and without reference to any books or other authority for guidance. According to this statement, a cashier must, in the exercise of his duties, sometimes display

    A. sincerity B. caution
    C. initiative D. courtesy

    6._____

7. To say that a cashier is METICULOUS in the performance of his duties is to say that he is

    A. extremely careful B. highly enthusiastic
    C. unusually fast D. prone to error

    7._____

8. The word NEGOTIABLE as used in business transactions means MOST NEARLY

   A. valueless
   B. transferable
   C. expensive
   D. profitable

9. An order which is RESCINDED is

   A. cancelled
   B. adopted
   C. clarified
   D. misunderstood

10. The word REMUNERATION means MOST NEARLY

    A. responsibility
    B. compensation
    C. complexity
    D. promotional opportunity

11. Assume that you are a cashier in an agency. Of the following, the MOST important reason why you should be courteous and tactful in dealing with visitors to your agency is that

    A. some of the visitors may show their appreciation of your courtesy by writing to your supervisor commending your work
    B. visitors who are treated courteously will probably treat you in the same manner
    C. visitors who are treated discourteously may ask your superior to take disciplinary action against you
    D. it is your responsibility to give the visitors a favorable impression of the agency

12. Assume that, as a cashier, you have been assigned the task of training a new employee in the work of collecting payments from the public.
    Of the following, the MOST effective technique to follow in training this employee is for you to

    A. encourage him by praising the work he has done correctly, but do not show him the mistakes he has made
    B. insist that he obey your instructions completely even if your instructions may not be clear to him
    C. encourage him to ask questions if he does not understand any of the work
    D. give him a complete understanding of his job by showing him the incorrect, as well as the correct ways of doing his work

13. Subtract the total of 9 quarters, 17 dimes and 12 nickels from the total of 6 half-dollars, 14 quarters, 8 dimes and 6 nickels.
    The *answer* is

    A. $2.05   B. $3.05   C. $3.15   D. $4.15

14. A certified check is one that

    A. states the purpose for which it is drawn
    B. has funds set aside to cover it by the bank upon which it is drawn
    C. is written by the bank upon which it is drawn
    D. requires the endorsements of both the payee and the maker before it can be cashed

15. Of the following, the MOST accurate description of a cashier's check is that it   15.____

    A. can be cashed only by the cashier of the Bank upon which it is drawn
    B. is drawn by a bank in payment for the services of one of its cashiers
    C. is drawn payable to the cashier of a bank by a depositor of the bank
    D. is drawn by a bank on its own funds and signed by its cashier

16. If, on a check, the amount payable expressed in words and the amount payable expressed in figures are not the same, then the amount payable is the   16.____

    A. amount in figures
    B. amount in words
    C. average of the two amounts
    D. lesser of the two amounts

Questions 17 - 20.

DIRECTIONS: Column I lists four different endorsements that a man named John Doe uses to endorse checks. Column II lists the names of five types of endorsements. In questions 17 to 20, for each endorsement listed in Column I, select the correct name in Column II by which that endorsement is generally known.

On your answer sheet, next to the number corresponding to each type of endorsement listed in Column I, write the capital letter preceding the name listed in Column II by which that endorsement is generally known.

COLUMN I		COLUMN II	
17. John Doe		A. blank	17.____
18. Without recourse John Doe		B. full	18.____
19. Pay to the order of Richard Roe John Doe		C. qualified	19.____
20. Pay to the order of City Bank for deposit only John Doe		D. conditional	20.____
		E. restricted	

Questions 21 - 25.

DIRECTIONS: Questions 21 to 25 are based on the following table.

COLLECTIONS BY CASHIERS FOR ONE WEEK

Name of Cashier	Monday	Tuesday	Wednesday	Thursday	Friday
Adams	$7487	$7435	$8864	$9264	$9876
Baker	9687	8643	8198	7415	8714
Taylor	7403	'6035	9722	9683	9512
Moore	6869	8212	9417	8933	9463
Foster	9129	9069	7734	8121	9596

21. Of the following, the day of the week on which the MOST money was collected is   21.____

    A. Tuesday   B. Wednesday
    C. Thursday   D. Friday

22. Of the following, the day of the week on which the LEAST money was collected is 22.___

    A. Monday B. Tuesday
    C. Wednesday D. Friday

23. The average amount collected per day by all the cashiers is 23.___

    A. less than $42,000
    B. between $42,000 and $42,500
    C. between $42,501 and $43,000
    D. more than $43,000

24. Foster's total collection for Monday, Tuesday and Friday are greater than Taylor's total collections for the same three days by MOST NEARLY 24.___

    A. 12%   B. 17%   C. 21%   D. 83%

25. The average amount collected per cashier on Wednesday 25.___

    A. was less than the average amount collected per cashier on Monday by $328
    B. was greater than the average amount collected per cashier on Monday by $672
    C. was less than the average amount collected per cashier on Thursday by $104
    D. was greater than the average amount collected per cashier on Thursday by $886

26. A bag contains 800 coins. Of these, 10 per cent are dimes, 30 per cent are nickels, and the rest are quarters. 26.___
    The amount of money in the bag is

    A. less than $150 B. between $150 and $300
    C. between $301 and $450 D. more than $450

27. On March 1, the revenue division of a city department counted $800,000. The money counted on March 2 was 10 per cent less than the money counted on March 1. If the money counted on March 3 was 10 per cent greater than the money counted on March 2, then the money counted on March 3 was 27.___

    A. $802,000 B. $792,000
    C. $720,000 D. $700,000

28. If one cashier can count a certain sum of money in 2 hours, and another cashier can count the same sum in 3 hours, then both cashiers working together can count this sum in 28.___

    A. 50 minutes B. 1 hour and 10 minutes
    C. 1 hour and 12 minutes D. 1 hour and 20 minutes

29. If the real estate tax is $4.11 per $100 of assessed valuation, the tax on real estate assessed at $19,500 is MOST NEARLY 29.___

    A. $47   B. $650   C. $800   D. $900

30. The tax collections in a tax office for the week ending January 11th were $468,693.80. If this amount was 20 per cent greater than the tax collections for the week ending January 4th, the tax collections for the week ending January 4th were MOST NEARLY 30.___

    A. $328,090   B. $375,000   C. $390,580   D. $393,705

31. Assume that the real estate tax rate is $4.08 per $100 of assessed valuation. If the tax on a house is $1,040.40, then the assessed valuation of the house is   31.____

   A. $25,500   B. $24,000
   C. $27,000   D. $28,500

32. Cashier X receives payments from 6 taxpayers every 15 minutes. Cashier Y receives payments from 15 taxpayers every half-hour. If Cashier X begins work at 9 a.m., and Cashier Y begins work at 9:30 a.m., the time at which the two Cashiers will have received payments from an equal number of taxpayers is   32.____

   A. 11 a.m.   B. 11:30 a.m.   C. 12 noon   D. 12:30 p.m.

33. The real estate tax on a piece of real property in a certain city is $1,082.40. If the assessed valuation of the property is $26,400, then the tax rate per $100 of assessed valuation is   33.____

   A. less than $4.05   B. between $4.05 and $4.08
   C. between $4.09 and $4.14   D. more than $4.14

34. If $300 is invested at simple interest so as to yield a return of $18 in 9 months, the amount of money that must be invested at the same rate of interest so as to yield a return of $120 in 6 months is   34.____

   A. $3000   B. $3300   C. $2000   D. $2300

35. Mr. Smith is reconciling his bank balance on November 15th by the use of the following information: 35.____
   Balance as per Bank Statement, October 31st - $15,932.20 Total Checks Outstanding, October 31st - 1,642.29 Total Deposits, November 1st to November 15th - 715.00 Total Checks Drawn, November 1st to November
   15th -   1,329.63
   According to the above information, the balance that Mr. Smith's checkbook should show as of the close of business on November 15th is MOST NEARLY

   A. $18,290   B. $16,647
   C. $13,675   D. $12,960

KEY (CORRECT ANSWERS)

1. C	11. D	21. D	31. A
2. A	12. C	22. B	32. B
3. A	13. B	23. C	33. C
4. C	14. B	24. C	34. A
5. C	15. D	25. B	35. C
6. C	16. B	26. A	
7. A	17. A	27. B	
8. B	18. C	28. C	
9. A	19. B	29. C	
10. B	20. E	30. C	

EXAMINATION SECTION
TEST 1

DIRECTIONS: Each question or incomplete statement is followed by several suggested answers or completions. Select the one that BEST answers the question or completes the statement. *PRINT THE LETTER OF THE CORRECT ANSWER IN THE SPACE AT THE RIGHT.*

1. The CHIEF purpose of a manual of *Instruction & Procedures for Money Room Employees* is to

   A. describe fully the grievance procedures available to money room employees
   B. describe methods of detecting counterfeit bills, coins, and tokens
   C. describe to money room employees the procedures that are to be used in their work
   D. help prepare money room employees to advance themselves to supervisory positions

2. The Transit, Highway, Bridge & Tunnel Authorities are created by the

   A. State Legislature   B. Public Service Commission
   C. City Council   D. Congress

3. The amount of money received and counted in the money room varies with the season of the year.
   Of the following, the CHIEF reason why the money counted is not the same in each season is that there is a seasonal change in the number of

   A. cashiers   B. collecting agents
   C. passengers   D. tollroad clerks

4. The assignments of bill cage cashiers in the money room are rotated so that each cashier verifies receipts from different tollroad clerks each day.
   The MOST important reason for rotating the cashiers' assignments is that

   A. the cashiers will become more familiar with various aspects of money room procedures
   B. each tollroad clerk remits a different amount of money each day
   C. collusion between cashiers and tollroad clerks is discouraged
   D. usually at least one cashier is absent every day

5. The one of the following for which a tollroad clerk would LEAST likely be held responsible is a counterfeit

   A. dollar bill   B. half-dollar
   C. nickel   D. token

6. Of the following, the MOST important precaution for a city employee to take when cashing his paycheck is to

   A. cash the check in a different bank each pay period
   B. endorse the check only when he is about to cash it
   C. insist that the check also be endorsed by the person cashing it
   D. ask the person who will cash the check to properly identify himself

7. In training a new cashier in safety procedures to be followed in the money room, it would be LEAST desirable to explain to him that

   A. the best safety device is a careful man
   B. most accidents are caused by carelessness
   C. it is more important to be careful during his training period than after he has completed his training
   D. he should always be alert to detect any possible hazards in the money room

8. The one of the following which is the SAFEST method for a cashier to use in lifting a heavy money bag is to

   A. bend his knees and back
   B. bend his knees and keep his back straight
   C. keep his knees and back straight
   D. keep his knees straight and bend his back

9. Money room procedures require that dimes, quarters, and half-dollars be bagged in amounts of $1000 each.
   The CHIEF justification for this procedure is that it simplifies the

   A. problem of storage of coins
   B. assigning of work to coin cashiers
   C. counting of money for bank deposit
   D. counting of remittances from tollroad clerks

10. One of the regulations in the money room requires that after $1000 in quarters has been counted and placed in a bag, the bag must be weighed.
    Of the following, the MOST important reason for weighing the bag is to

    A. eliminate the necessity for the bank to recount the money
    B. determine if an error has been made in counting the money
    C. insure against overloading the money truck carrying the money to the bank
    D. make certain that there are no counterfeit coins in the bag

Questions 11-17.

DIRECTIONS: Questions 11 through 17 are to be answered on the basis of the following information.

$100 in pennies weighs 68 pounds; $50 in nickels weighs 11 pounds; $1000 in silver of any denomination weighs 54 pounds; and 1000 tokens valued at $1.50 each weigh 3 pounds, 14 ounces.

11. The weight of $77 in pennies is MOST NEARLY _____ pounds.

    A. 52   B. 48   C. 54   D. 60

12. If the tokens in a bag weigh 1 pound, 15 ounces, then the value of these tokens is

    A. $500   B. $750   C. $50   D. $850

13. The contents of a bag containing halves, dimes, and quarters weigh 38 pounds. 13.____
    The amount of money in the bag is MOST NEARLY

    A. $234   B. $380   C. $760   D. $704

14. The weight of the contents of a bag containing $35 in pennies, $41 in nickels, and $730 14.____
    in silver is

    A. less than 60 pounds
    B. between 60 pounds and 70 pounds
    C. between 71 pounds and 80 pounds
    D. more than 80 pounds

15. In a bag containing 1000 coins, half of the coins are nickels and the other half are dimes. 15.____
    The weight of the coins in the bag is MOST NEARLY _____ pounds.

    A. 8   B. 11   C. 5   D. 75

16. A bag contains $25 in pennies, $200 in quarters, $250 in dimes, and an unspecified 16.____
    amount in nickels.
    If the weight of all the coins in the bag is 60 pounds, then the amount of money, in nickels, is

    A. less than $80   B. between $80 and $90
    C. between $91 and $100   D. more than $100

17. A bag contains $780 in nickels, dimes, and quarters. 17.____
    Of the total number of coins in the bag, 10 percent are dimes, 20 percent are nickels,
    and the rest are quarters. If there are 400 dimes in the bag, then the weight of all the
    coins is

    A. less than 25 pounds
    B. between 25 pounds and 35 pounds
    C. between 36 pounds and 45 pounds
    D. more than 45 pounds

18. 27/64 expressed as a percent is 18.____

    A. 40.6250%   B. 42.1875%   C. 43.7500%   D. 45.3133%

19. $40 reduced by 3/8 of itself is 19.____

    A. $25   B. $65   C. $15   D. $55

20. $1,525.62 minus $397.29 is 20.____

    A. $1137.43   B. $1237.33   C. $1128.33   D. $1127.33

21. 12 1/2 minus 6 1/4 is 21.____

    A. 6 1/4   B. 5 3/4   C. 6 1/2   D. 5 1/2

22. 416 machine bolts $3.75 per hundred will cost 22.____

    A. $.156   B. $156.000   C. $1.560   D. $15.600

23. 21.70 divided by 1.75 equals 23.____

    A. 124.0   B. 12.4   C. 1.24   D. 0.124

24. The number 0.03125 reduced to a common fraction is

    A. 3/64 B. 1/16 C. 1/32 D. 1/13

25. 7/8 divided by 2/7 is

    A. 1/4 B. 3 1/16 C. 9/15 D. 4 1/16

26. Men's white linen handkerchiefs cost $1.29 for 3.
    The cost per dozen handkerchiefs is

    A. $7.75 B. $3.87 C. $14.48 D. $5.16

27. 357 is 6% of

    A. 2142 B. 5950 C. 4140 D. 5900

28. 572 divided by .52 is

    A. 1100 B. 110 C. 11.10 D. 11.00

29. The number of decimal places in the product of 0.4266 and 0.3333 is

    A. 8 B. 6 C. 4 D. 2

30. 72 divided by 0.009 is

    A. 0.125 B. 800 C. 8000 D. 80

31. Add 5 hrs. 13 min., 3 hrs. 49 min., and 14 min.
    The sum is _____ hrs. _____ min.

    A. 8; 16 B. 9; 16 C. 9; 76 D. 8; 6

32. The cost of 7 3/4 tons of coal at $20.16 per ton is

    A. $15.12 B. $151.20 C. $141.12 D. $156.24

33. A salesman gets a commission of 6% on his sales.
    If he wants his commission to amount to $72, he will have to sell merchandise totaling

    A. $142 B. $1200 C. $120 D. $12

34. The sum of 90.79, 79.09, 97.90, and 9.97 is

    A. 277.75 B. 278.56 C. 276.94 D. 277.93

35. John Doe borrowed $225,000.00 for 5 years at 8 1/2%.
    The annual interest charge was

    A. $15,750 B. $15,550 C. $19,125 D. $39,375

KEY (CORRECT ANSWERS)

1.	C	16.	B
2.	A	17.	D
3.	C	18.	B
4.	C	19.	A
5.	D	20.	C
6.	B	21.	A
7.	C	22.	D
8.	B	23.	B
9.	C	24.	C
10.	B	25.	B
11.	A	26.	D
12.	B	27.	B
13.	D	28.	A
14.	C	29.	A
15.	A	30.	C

31. B
32. D
33. B
34. A
35. C

TEST 2

DIRECTIONS: Each question or incomplete statement is followed by several suggested answers or completions. Select the one that BEST answers the question or completes the statement. *PRINT THE LETTER OF THE CORRECT ANSWER IN THE SPACE AT THE RIGHT.*

1. Which number is one more than 4000?
   A. 3099   B. 3900   C. 4001   D. 3999

2. What does MCCXII mean?
   A. 712   B. 512   C. 802   D. 1212

3. What is fifty-two ten-thousandths written as a decimal?
   A. 52,010,000   B. .052   C. .0052   D. .00052

4. What is .127 expressed as a percent?
   A. 12.7%   B. 1.27%   C. 12 7/100%   D. 12 1/2%

5. What is seventy billion forty million sixty in figures?
   A. 70,400,060,000   B. 70,040,600,000
   C. 70,040,000,060   D. 70,040,000,600

6. What is the equivalent decimal of the fraction 7/8%?
   A. .875   B. .675   C. .575   D. .785

7. What is the common fraction equivalent (in its lowest terms) of .58 1/3%?
   A. 5/12   B. 174/300   C. 175/100   D. 7/12

8. The Health Department reported that 8 out of 12 children had the measles this spring. What fraction shows what proportion of the children had measles?
   A. 8/20   B. 2/3   C. 1/8   D. 1/12

9. The State census report showed 10,308,252 people in the State. How should this number be written when rounded to the nearest million?
   A. 11,000,000   B. 10,309,000
   C. 10,308,000   D. 10,000,000

10. When 3/4% of the people of Seattle have been vaccinated for smallpox, what fraction has been vaccinated?
    A. 3/400   B. 1/75   C. 3/4   D. 4/300

11. What percent of 33 1/3 is 8 1/3?
    A. 66 2/3%   B. 4%   C. 25%   D. 10%

2 (#2)

12. The grades received on a clerical examination were as follows: one received a grade of 90; three received 85; four, 80; two, 75; six, 70; five, 65; two, 60; one, 55; one, 50; one, 45; one, 40; one, 30; and one, 25.
    What was the average grade on the examination to the nearest tenth percent?

    A. 85.0%   B. 77.2%   C. 72.7%   D. 66.4%

    12._____

13. A clerk saved 16 2/3% of his salary.
    If his salary was $1800 a month, how many years and months did he work to save $13,500?

    A. 3 years, 9 months   B. 3 years, 6 months
    C. 4 years   D. 3 years, 3 months

    13._____

14. Folders, each containing the same number of sheets, are filed alphabetically in a 4-drawer cabinet. The inside length of each drawer is 35 inches, and all 4 drawers are packed full. Filed under A are 43 folders occupying 7 inches.
    How many folders are there in the whole cabinet?

    A. 20   B. 215   C. 860   D. 645

    14._____

15. A machine operator is paid at the rate of $22.20 per hour if his hourly average production is 250 written bills. For any day in which his hourly average is below 250, his hourly rate of pay is reduced by one-sixth.
    What would be his pay for a seven-hour day in which he produced 1715 written bills?

    A. $129.50   B. $136.90   C. $151.70   D. $155.40

    15._____

16. A stenographer transcribes her notes at the rate of one line typed in ten seconds.
    At this rate, how long (in minutes and seconds) will it take her to transcribe notes which will require seven pages of typing, 25 lines to the page?
    _____ minutes, _____ seconds.

    A. 29; 10   B. 17; 50   C. 40; 10   D. 20; 30

    16._____

17. During one week, a personnel agency receives 192 applications on Monday, 213 on Tuesday, 218 on Wednesday, 215 on Thursday, 102 on Friday, and 194 on Saturday.
    If the agency has seven branch offices, what is the daily average number of applications received in each office for the entire week?

    A. 29   B. 27   C. 189   D. 47

    17._____

18. Pencils used in an office may be bought at the price of two for 10 cents or, when bought in large quantities, at the price of $13.80 for six dozen.
    What is the saving per dozen when pencils are bought at the lower rate?

    A. $.70   B. $1.00   C. $3.70   D. $7.80

    18._____

19. If retirement deductions from salaries are increased from 3 1/2% to 5%, what is the monthly amount of the increase in the deduction from an $18,000 salary?

    A. $15.30   B. $52.50   C. $78.30   D. $22.50

    19._____

20. A man invested $75,000 in a new business enterprise. The first year, he lost .16 2/3 of his original investment. The next year, he made a profit of 1/8 of his net worth at the beginning of that year.
His net worth at the end of the second year was what part of his original investment?

    A. 6 1/4%   B. 75%   C. 80%   D. 93 3/4%

21. 0.16 3/4 written as a percent is

    A. 16 3/4%   B. 16.3/4%   C. 0.016 3/4%   D. 0.0016 3/4%

22. $40 reduced by 3/8 of itself is

    A. $25   B. $65   C. $15   D. $55

23. $1,296.53 minus $264.87 is

    A. $1,232.76   B. $1,032.76   C. $1,031.66   D. $1,132.53

24. 12 1/2 minus 6 1/4 is

    A. 5 3/4   B. 6 1/4   C. 6 1/2   D. 5 1/2

25. A desk is marked $98, 20% 30 days, or $98, 30% 15 days cash.
If it is paid for in cash immediately on delivery, the amount paid is

    A. $66.84   B. $63.70   C. $68.40   D. $68.60

26. Add 1/4, 7/12, 3/8, 1/2, 5/6.

    A. 2 1/2   B. 2 13/24   C. 2 3/4   D. 2 15/24

27. A floor is 25 ft. wide by 36 ft. long.
To cover this floor with carpet will require _____ square yards.

    A. 100   B. 300   C. 900   D. 25

28. A salesman gets a commission of 4% on his sales.
If he wants his commission to amount to $40, he will have to sell merchandise totaling

    A. $160   B. $10   C. $1000   D. $100

29. Add 5 hours, 13 minutes; 3 hours, 49 minutes; and 14 minutes.
The sum is _____ hours, _____ minutes.

    A. 8; 16   B. 9; 16   C. 9; 76   D. 8; 6

30. John Doe borrowed $425,000 for 5 years at 9 1/2%.
The annual interest charge was

    A. $25,750   B. $35,750   C. $40,375   D. $42,950

31. 72 divided by .009 is

    A. .125   B. 800   C. 8000   D. 80

32. 345 locks at $4.15 per hundred will cost

    A. $.1432   B. $1.4320   C. $14.32   D. $143.20

33. The number which, when decreased by 1/5 of itself equals 132, is   33.____
    A. 165	B. 198	C. 98	D. 88

34. 285 is 5% of   34.____
    A. 1700	B. 7350	C. 1750	D. 5700

35. A store sold suits for $65 each. The suits cost $50 each. The percentage of increase of selling price over cost is   35.____
    A. 40%	B. 33 1/2%	C. 33 1/3%	D. 30%

KEY (CORRECT ANSWERS)

1. C	16. A
2. D	17. B
3. C	18. A
4. A	19. D
5. C	20. D
6. A	21. A
7. D	22. A
8. B	23. C
9. D	24. B
10. A	25. D
11. C	26. B
12. D	27. A
13. A	28. C
14. C	29. B
15. A	30. C

31. C
32. C
33. A
34. D
35. D

www.ingramcontent.com/pod-product-compliance
Lightning Source LLC
Chambersburg PA
CBHW082041300426
44117CB00015B/2563